75

THE ROAD TO DICTATORSHIP

Germany 1918-1933

Translated from the German by
LAWRENCE WILSON

Ten Contributions by
    Th. Eschenburg
    E. Fraenkel
    K. Sontheimer
    E. Matthias
    R. Morsey
    O. K. Flechtheim
    K. D. Bracher
    H. Krausnick
    H. Rothfels
    E. Kogon

OSWALD WOLFF
London
1970

First published in Germany by
R. Piper & Co. Verlag, Munich, 1962
© 1962 by R. Piper Verlag
© 1964 for English translation by Oswald Wolff (Publishers) Ltd., London
Reprinted 1970

PRINTED IN GREAT BRITAIN BY
WILLIAM LEWIS (PRINTERS) LTD
CARDIFF

CONTENTS

THEODOR ESCHENBURG
*The Collapse of Democratic Régimes between the
First and the Second World Wars*   7

ERNST FRAENKEL
Historical Handicaps of German Parliamentarianism   25

KURT SONTHEIMER
Anti-democratic Thought in the Weimar Republic   39

ERICH MATTHIAS
Social Democracy and the Power in the State   57

RUDOLF MORSEY
The Centre Party between the Fronts   75

OSSIP K. FLECHTHEIM
The Role of the Communist Party   93

KARL DIETRICH BRACHER
*The Technique of the National Socialist Seizure
of Power*   111

HELMUT KRAUSNICK
Stages of Co-ordination   127

HANS ROTHFELS
Resistance begins   143

EUGEN KOGON
Lessons for Tomorrow   159

These essays were originally
broadcast in the Third Programme of the *Norddeutscher
Rundfunk*

THEODOR ESCHENBURG

The Collapse of Democratic Régimes between the First and the Second World Wars

Professor Theodor Eschenburg was born in
1904. He studied history, national economy
and political law in Tübingen and Berlin
and took his degree in 1928. From 1930 to
1945 he held managing positions in industry.
For some years after the war he was State
Commissioner for Refugees in Württemberg-
Hohenzollern. Since 1952 he has been Professor of Political Science at Tübingen
University. He has published a number of
books on historical and contemporary political subjects.

In speaking here about the European democracies between the two world wars, I am deliberately going to exclude Germany. But it cannot be my task either to portray the testing and failure of democracy in detail; I am going to confine myself to pointing out some typical phenomena and important turning-points. For this I must use a schematic approach which I realise is no more than an aid to study and assessment.

If we use the internal structure of states as a method of division, *three zones* can be distinguished in Europe before the First World War. In the *first zone* lie the democratic states of Western Europe—the British Isles and on the Continent France, the Scandinavian countries, Belgium, Holland and Switzerland. In these countries a democratic constitution existed before 1914. The formation of governments lay in the hands of the parliaments and in the monarchies the heads of state no longer functioned as political rulers. The upper houses had been defeudalised or had lost considerably in importance compared with the elected representatives of the people. Universal equal suffrage had been or shortly was to be introduced. The decisive steps towards democratisation had been taken in a period of great economic expansion and neither economic crises nor military defeats had shaken the new system of government. Social legislation was as yet barely included among the duties of the state and was making a slow beginning. It was not yet in the centre of political controversy and the state still had no need to make material demands on its citizens; one has only to remember the rates of income tax in those times which to us today seem inconceivably low. Up to the outbreak of war the French had not been able to make up their minds to introduce an income tax at all. An essential fact was that in these countries the clergy of the Protestant Churches supported or at least did not resist the process of democratisation and that accordingly in the part-Catholic, part-Protestant countries—Belgium, Holland, Switzerland and also to a certain degree in France—the Catholic clergy respected this development and were merely concerned to maintain the Church's position in the controversy with "Liber-

9

alism" and "Laicism". These were the states of bourgeois democracy to which North America belonged as the only country outside Europe. With the exception of France none of them had experienced any severe internal crisis during the course of democratisation and France had quickly surmounted hers. In these countries democracy had taken root, its principles were no longer a subject of controversy, while the small states had no dreams of hegemony and therefore did not pursue an active foreign policy so that this question, too, was not a subject of internal political dissension. All the above-mentioned states can therefore be called stable democracies.

The structure of the constitution in Spain, Portugal, Italy and Greece, which must also be included in the *first zone*, was likewise at that time more or less democratic in a formal sense. But these countries lacked the social conditions necessary for democracy to take root. In varying degrees they had preserved their feudal character. A high proportion of illiteracy, great differences in wealth and the lack of a middle class impeded the process of democratisation which was interrupted and even imperilled by revolutionary outbursts. An exception was Italy although social conditions here were similar to those in the other three countries. But in Italy the instability characteristic of the other states was mitigated by the supreme parliamentary skill of the Liberal Giolitti who was several times Prime Minister between 1895 and 1914. In all these states the Catholic clergy, supported by and supporting the feudal upper classes, attempted to stem and even to reverse the democratic process as a defence against liberal and still more against socialist revolutionary tendencies. On the other hand, as elsewhere the use of democratic procedures was only possible in these countries thanks to the great economic upsurge which the world had experienced in more than fifty years of peace. Thus in the first zone the stable confront the unstable democracies.

The *second zone* includes the so-called "old legitimist states", the constitutional monarchies of Germany and Austria-Hungary —in this context I am leaving Turkey and Russia as a whole out of account. The heritage of absolutism, though restricted by the constitution, had survived in these countries. The upper chamber still retained a mainly feudal character. The monarch was also the ruler, besides being the military commander-in-chief and master of the administration. In the sphere of legislation the parliament was only one partner among three. The Swiss historian Werner Näf has called the Bismarckian *Kaiser-reich* "a monarchy with democratic additions". In both states, thanks to a highly qualified judiciary and a homogeneous and equally well qualified bureaucracy, strict constitutionalism prevailed. If the western and northern frontiers of Germany and the western frontier of Austria-Hungary separated the democratic from the constitutionally authoritarian sphere, the zone of European constitutionalism, with as prerequisite the separation of powers, stretched to the eastern frontier of Germany and the eastern and southern frontiers of the Habsburg Empire. Thanks to the existence of a ruling sovereign and a uniform and well functioning bureaucracy the organisation of these states was stable. On the other hand there was instability in Austria-Hungary owing to the possibility of a crisis arising from the centrifugal forces of its diverse nationalities and in Germany from the steady growth in parliament of Social Democracy which at that time was directed both against the monarchy and the middle class.

The *third zone* is very much harder to determine. In his *Weltgeschichte der neuesten Zeit* the Swiss historian Salis places its frontiers on the Elbe and the Danube. This seems to me too far west. But it may be difficult to find a geographical demarcation line at all. This is the area of East, Central and South-East Europe with a marked or mainly agrarian character in which class conceptions and feudal social conditions still strongly predominate. The idea of the constitutional state encounters and impinges on them without being able to prevail over the feudal social order as it has done in Central and Western Europe. The economic prosperity of the West penetrates this area only very slightly or hardly at all. Even where the process of industrialisation has started, the feudal order remains or the middle-class *entrepreneurs* attempt to adapt it to their ends. The Churches are authoritarian or feudal in outlook, to say the least anti-democratic; the percentage of illiteracy is very high. To this zone belong those parts of the Russian state with Russian population which have inherited western conceptions from their past, in other words the Baltic provinces and Poland. Finland occupies a special position in so far as it exercises a certain degree of autonomy, though in the course of time this has been restricted by the Russians, and also because it has close connections with the Scandinavian countries owing to its geographical position and to the fact that, despite growing self-awareness on the part of the Finnish population, its Swedish upper class still holds the political reins. To this zone also belong the Balkan states which with their predominantly Greek Orthodox population arose during the nineteenth century in the European part of the Turkish Empire. These are young states, in some cases formerly ruled autocratically by foreign dynasties, which owing to their national conflicts and lack of consolidation were in a very unstable condition. Characteristic of this zone is the mixture of nationalities which produced a variety of nationalisms on a small scale. Austria projected into this zone as a multi-racial state with supranational power. One must therefore distinguish between a democratic zone, a zone of constitutional monarchy and a mainly authoritarian zone.

The peace of Brest-Litowsk at the end of the First World War in 1918 led to the separation of areas marked by European conceptions from Russia, namely Poland, the Baltic provinces and Finland. These countries were thereby preserved from bolshevisation. According to the German conception, constitutional monarchies were to be created in this area with a more or less strong dependency on Vienna and Berlin, a conception which was powerfully influenced by fear of the social agrarian revolution which was threatening from the East. Leaving for a moment all national considerations out of account, from a purely organisational point of view the transition from feudal authoritarianism to a constitutional monarchy would probably have proceeded more smoothly and would thus have been less subject to crises, because in this way considerably less demands would have been made on the population than through democracy. But in the ruling circles in Germany at that time less interest was shown in constitutional adaptation coupled with a high degree of autonomy than in military control and economic exploitation. In articles in the *Frankfurter Zeitung* which appeared in 1915, in other words before the Bolshevist revolution, Max Weber had recommended considerate treatment by Germany of the western Slav states so as not to drive them on to the side of Russia.

Germany was forced to abandon this conception through the military defeat in the summer and autumn of 1918. Its place was taken by Woodrow Wilson's plan, President of the victorious United States, as expressed in his fourteen points : right of self-determination and democracy for the peoples under foreign rule. It was not until 1917 that the First World War received its ideological stamp and the impulse came from the United States which entered the war in that year as a struggle between democracy and despotism. The victory of the allies was counted therefore as a victory of democracy.

The new countries in the authoritarian-feudal zone which had arisen owing to the weakness of the powers which had previously dominated them—Germany, Austria-Hungary and Russia—would have had little alternative than to set up democratic regimes even without Wilson's backing. In these areas there were no pretenders to the throne who passed as legitimate. The feudal upper class had been discredited owing to collaboration with the formerly ruling powers. The Bolshevists had no chance of success because opposition to Russian Communism was no less strong than it had been to Russian Tsardom. There was no reason for a dictatorship because the big neighbours had been weakened through defeat and revolution and there were no opponents left in the international field. On the other hand, Austria-Hungary, whose peoples he had cautiously promised only autonomy, would have collapsed even without Wilson's push. After the death of the Emperor Franz Joseph it would have been impossible to hold the state together in the event of defeat. Equally, the one-time Russian territories which had been split off at the Peace of Brest-Litowsk would have achieved their own independence without much difficulty, though perhaps in a slightly different form. Germany had given the impulse to their becoming separate states, but was no longer in a position to support them. The traditional and stable democracies of Western Europe in the first zone, namely Britain, Belgium, Holland, Switzerland and the three Scandinavian countries, had been able to pass the necessary social measures which material or political conditions after the war demanded and continue their constitutional development in the direction of full democratisation. In these states no question arose as to the fitness of traditionally democratic institutions to bear the new burdens imposed on the state in the post-war period in so far as the democratic form of constitution was held responsible for increased expenditure and taxation.

Conditions in the countries of East and South-East Europe were entirely different. Here on the one hand new states arose like Poland and Finland, the Baltic countries Estonia, Latvia and Lithuania, and Czechoslovakia, and on the other, states already in existence like Rumania and Yugoslavia acquired such an increase of territory that they were faced with barely soluble problems of integration. All these newly created states in East, Central and South-East Europe either received a parliamentary and democratic constitution after the western pattern or adapted their existing authoritarian forms of government accordingly. They were *improvised democracies* lacking the intellectual preparation or the stages of development which the traditional democracies had known. The switch from a feudal and authoritarian system to a democratic order with responsibilities for social welfare had taken place without any transition. In the new states the upper classes, in so far as they had existed, were stripped of power. There were no experienced politicians and no experienced civil service. The process of integration was strongly inhibited by the existence of, in some cases, very large national minorities which brought their full weight to bear thanks to proportional representation. The new states were carved out of large economic areas and their isolation confronted them with difficult economic and social problems as well as with the necessity of bearing almost alone the internal burdens which had resulted from the war.

Bulgaria, Hungary and Austria were so heavily truncated that their ability to maintain economic independence was endangered. In these states the question of how to preserve their newly created political independence was also a source of fear. Though the restoration of Austria-Hungary was very improbable, Russia and Germany still existed and might one day press for the return of what they had lost. In particular, the states bordering on Soviet Russia lived in continual concern at its internal political developments and their possible international consequences. Apart from some exceptions which I shall discuss later, there was also a widespread though varying lack of the political and social prerequisites for a democratic order. In most of these states the parliamentary democratic system failed in the course of the next fifteen years and the threatened breakdown of government threw up dictatorships of varying kinds. These dictatorships were set up by military men, leading politicians or by the monarchs themselves and brought about by more or less overt *coups d'état* and also by uprisings of organised movements.

We can speak here of functional dictatorships whose task it was simply to keep the state intact. Some of them were even educational dictatorships which were only intended to last until the political and social conditions of stability were created. These dictatorships were less concerned with ideological goals or with giving the state a definite form, but merely with keeping the state alive that had been so unexpectedly resurrected or enlarged. The dictatorships were therefore of a more or less moderate kind. The constitutional structure, in so far as it had become established, was maintained or only slightly interfered with. In many cases these dictatorships were strongly anti-Fascist, as in Estonia and Rumania where Fascist organisations existed and were combated by the authoritarian governments. Most of these dictatorships had no ideological slant and were not based on organised movements. They became established as institutions in Estonia and Latvia and also to some extent in Poland where the initially weak presidential powers were strengthened. But there was at least a chance that the democratic system might be restored if social conditions developed sufficiently.

Four exceptions to this trend towards dictatorship must be briefly referred to. In Finland democracy survived, even in the Second World War, despite the alliance with National Socialist Germany. Finland was the only democratic state which fought on Germany's side and, apart from Japan, the only one which preserved its independence against Hitler. Finland also survived after 1945 against victorious Soviet Russia. In this connection it must be remembered that the Swedish upper stratum, which comprises 10 per cent of the population, was displaced but not suppressed by the Finnish middle class and the steadily growing Finnish intelligentsia during the formation and early development of the state. But in this country there existed a lively liberal and democratic tradition of anti-authoritarian character. It was allied with an anti-Russian attitude and Scandinavian influence was also at work in it. There were no important differences between the democratic thought of Sweden and Finland. In Finland, too, an ultra-democratic constitution had been introduced after the First World War. In 1930, the constitutional powers of the President were strengthened, mainly under pressure from the peasant Fascist Lappo Movement which had been founded at the instigation of the Lutheran clergy and disappeared from the scene after fulfilling its purpose by putting

through a ban on the Communist Party at the same time as an
increase in the powers of the President. The man who had
brought the Lappo Movement into office, the astute and aged
Prime Minister Svinhufvud, dissociated himself from it. Its anti-
democratic programme ceased to find much support and in
1938 it suffered a crushing defeat at the elections.

Democracy also survived in Czechoslovakia until Hitler
destroyed it in 1938. In this, the most strongly industrialised
area of former Austria-Hungary, the social basis of a democratic
system was already in existence. Among the West Slav peoples
the Czechs had the lowest percentage of illiteracy. In Bohemia
even under the Habsburgs the middle and higher ranks of the
civil service were well trained, experienced and reliable and in
the new state with its minorities they became a stabilising factor.
Here there was a strong middle-class and in the Czech *bourgeoisie*
a democratic tradition had developed in the struggle against the
German predominance in the Austrian monarchy. The existence
of a freely elected parliament, which the East European states
had not possessed, offered an opportunity for this. The minorities which were relatively liberal in the political, though less so
in the economic and social sphere did not have so disintegrating
an effect as in Poland—their pressure brought the Czech parties
closer together. Above all, the integrating force emanating from
Masaryk, the actual founder of this state which was not included in Wilson's original conception, should not be underestimated. It was he who held the state together in masterly
fashion, a statesman deserving the highest respect, the Franz-
Joseph figure, as it were, of Czechoslovakia. The French historian Baumont speaks of the *dictature du respect*. A Fascist movement was suppressed in 1933. Of the five parties of the German
minority one was Fascist: the National Socialist Party. In
Slovakia there existed an authoritarian movement for autonomy
led by the clergy and organised on Fascist lines. But this only
became effective through Hitler in 1938. Thus democracy in
Czechoslovakia was stable.

Social conditions in Austria were similar to those in Czechoslovakia. Both areas had, after all, been the ones with the
strongest western connections in the old monarchy. But political
conditions were completely different. At first, Austria did not
want to become an independent state, but it had to. The
Catholic, primarily peasant population, particularly the clergy,

had had a much more positive attitude to the monarchy, with its Catholic ruling house, than had been the case in the German Reich. Even after the collapse, therefore, they favoured an authoritarian regime. On the other hand, Austrian Social Democracy before the First World War had belonged to the left wing of the Second International. Whereas in Bismarck's *Kaiser-reich* the Centre and Social Democratic Parties had been discriminated against in varying degrees and had therefore often co-operated, later agreeing on a common governmental policy under the Weimar Republic, in Austria the old sharp contrast continued and even became more acute. Moreover, the Austrian Social Democrats were supporters and the Catholics under Seipel were opponents of union with Germany. Union would probably have had a calming effect in Austria and certainly also a moderating influence on the *reichdeutsch* parties, but at that time it was not practicable, particularly from an international point of view, as it would have made Hungary, with her strong revisionist aims, a direct neighbour of Germany and Czechoslovakia would have been closely surrounded with German territory. Fascist Italy also opposed union on account of South Tirol and for that reason gave intensive support to the authoritarian efforts of the Austrian Christian Socialists. On the other hand, the Austrian National Socialists were in the main enthusiastic for union. In Austria, Fascism was both a model and an opponent. In March, 1933, by means of a *coup d'état* based on strong para-military formations, Dollfuss created a dictatorial regime in the form of a "Christian corporate state" which was opposed both to "red democracy" and "red Vienna" and also to union with National Socialist Germany. Austria was more an ideological than a functional dictatorship.

The fourth exception is Hungary. Here, apart from one short interruption, the feudal constitutional monarchy survived the world war and the collapse of the Danube monarchy as the only remaining one in Europe. The peace treaty took from Hungary two thirds of her former territory, but for that very reason the old rule was preserved. The Magyars lost considerable parts of their country, but thereby they also lost their opponents in the Banate, Transylvania, Croatia and Slovakia whom they had previously dominated. This monarchy without a monarch was based on the lesser nobility and the clergy. A democratic opposition could not arise because there was no

2—TRTD

educated urban middle-class and the peasants were also un-
educated and unorganised.

So in the course of fifteen years, more or less unideological
dictatorships arose in East, Central and South-East Europe
which before 1914 had been the authoritarian, feudal zone.
Admittedly, these dictatorships were brought about or furthered
by ideological impulses, for instance by the Catholic clergy in
Lithuania and the Greek-Orthodox in Rumania, or they opposed
certain political tendencies, particularly the Socialists, in part
just because of their strictly democratic views, as for example in
Estonia and Latvia, and also in Bulgaria. But no one-sided
totalitarian ideology prevailed. With their improvised democratic constitutions the states had been overstrained at a pre-
democratic stage of their social organisation and had only been
able to resolve this stress in an authoritarian manner. Granted
peaceful development and a steadily favourable economic situation a closer approximation to the West European democracies
might have been expected in time. These kinds of dictatorship
were intermediate constitutional stages between a feudal, authoritarian and a democratic system. Apart from Pilsudski of Poland,
they were characterised by a lack of charismatic *Führer*-figures.
But even Pilsudski's death did not plunge Poland into a political
crisis. Equally characteristic were the royal dictatorships of
South-East Europe where the monarchs ruled with interchange-
able prime ministers.

This process did not extend to the areas abutting on or be-
longing to Western Europe which were at a higher stage of social
development and were able to make use of a political tradition.
Finland and Czechoslovakia remained democracies, Hungary a
constitutional monarchy. It was only in Austria, where the
natural course of union with Germany was barred, that democracy turned into an ideological dictatorship. Austria alone was
too small and economically too feeble to work out her extreme
internal conflicts in a democratic way.

Italy was widely considered the model of an ideological
dictatorship on a *bourgeois* pattern. This country had suffered
severely from the First World War and of the allied Great
Powers had come off worst under the Peace Treaty. On the
allied side, therefore, it felt the consequences of the war more
strongly than any. Giolitti had opposed Italy's entry into the
war for good reasons, fearing that war would overstrain the

country economically and socially. One of his propagandist opponents was Mussolini who had been thrown out of the Socialist Party for supporting participation in the war. After the war, Mussolini founded a movement for social renewal which to start with worked with a variety of passionate, but vague catchwords; it exploited the dissatisfaction of wide sections of the population with the economic distress to attack democratic institutions and attracted to itself revolutionary intellectuals in particular, but also ex-soldiers who were finding their way back into civil life with difficulty as well as the more intelligent of the small peasants, or at least those people who were not organised in the Marxist parties, but were suffering from inflation and unemployment. Industry and the big landowners supported Mussolini's movement from fear of left-wing radicalism. Contrary to their expectations, the Russian Communists had not succeeded in igniting revolution in even one country, apart from Hungary and even there only temporarily. But if there had been a chance anywhere, the best chance would have been in Italy immediately after the war. By 1922, this danger had almost ceased to exist as the Socialist parties were fighting fiercely among themselves. But deliberate exaggeration of the danger was a powerful instrument of propaganda in Mussolini's hands. His antiliberal, antidemocratic slogans found readier credence among the middle-class in that the workers who, in so far as they were illiterate had previously been denied the vote, appeared as the beneficiaries of universal suffrage, first introduced in 1919. This shift in the distribution of power induced the middle-class to surrender their old principles in order to be safe from Socialism and Communism.

Mussolini opened, as it were, the antiliberal and antidemocratic struggle in Europe which started in the early 1920's. Liberalism and democracy only seemed worth achieving or maintaining so long as, thanks mainly to the class suffrage and the suffrage according to income, they seemed like privileges of the upper stratum. The attitude of the clergy was to a great extent undecided. The Fascist movement became a power-seeking organisation, organised on military and strictly hierarchical lines, at the bidding of a charismatic leader who through it had a private army at his disposal. It had no political programme like Communism, from whose methods and organisation it borrowed much, and this was replaced by a pseudo-historical nostalgia harking back to the greatness of Ancient Rome and the splendours of the Renaissance and intended to arouse hopes of their revival. Basically the movement was opportunistic and only interested in power as such. It therefore opposed the power-holders of that time with their institutions. In this form and this connection Fascism was a new phenomenon in Europe; it exploited the downcast mood of the Italian people who had gone to war and, though not among the conquered, had achieved—which was equally depressing—no tangible successes and even had to suffer severely under the burdens of war.

In fact, the state fell a prey to persistent and increasingly serious functional disorders. Proportional representation, which had been introduced after the war, had made the formation of governments much harder. Frequent changes of government continually weakened governmental authority. So there arose in Italy under Mussolini the first non-Communist ideological and institutionalised dictatorship. But it was not until after the seizure of power that the Fascist movement received its ideological stamp, and then for opportunistic reasons the new goals varied considerably from the old ones which had served the achievement of power. One of the strongest stimuli of the Fascist movement were Mussolini's international demands that Italy should become the dominating power in the Mediterranean, as Ancient Rome had been. After the seizure of power, the ceaseless repetition of these imperialistic claims served to hold the Fascist state together. At first, in fact, Mussolini had pursued a very cautious foreign policy in order to protect the still fluid internal conditions from foreign risks. It was not until 1936 that, relying on and at the same time vying with Hitler, he began his foreign adventures.

More or less on the Italian model, though varying greatly in size, similar organisations arose in most European states, even in some traditionally democratic countries, but only one, namely the German, achieved success.

In Spain and Portugal developments were different than in Italy. Spain had not taken part in the war and therefore did not have to suffer from its consequences, but it did suffer severely from economic backwardness and the sharp differences between the working population and the feudal forces, particularly the big landowners and the Church. A democratic compromise was hardly possible here. Weak governments confronted strong extra-parliamentary forces the anarcho-syndicalist movement on the one hand and the officers' juntas on the other. Efforts by the Catalonians to achieve autonomy threatened to endanger the unity of the state. Since the restoration of the monarchy in 1874, Spain had been in a state of latent civil war. The only possibilities seemed to be a radical Socialist or a conservative and Catholic dictatorship. The régime of General Primo de Rivera from 1923 to 1930 was a kind of royal dictatorship. In 1924, to secure his power on the pattern of Italian Fascism he founded a government party, the Patriot Union, but it did not find wide support. In 1931, a year after Primo de Rivera had resigned at the request of the king, the monarchy was overthrown. The republican governments did not succeed in stabilising conditions either. In 1933, the Falange was founded as a counter-movement to the Syndicalists. It was a Fascist organisation, but with radical Socialist, left-wing Catholic and republican tendencies. Its aim was the one-party state, but it lacked a charismatic leader and at the start was of no importance. To begin with, General Franco's military revolt took place independently of the Falange. Franco was a conservative monarchist with strong clerical leanings. His aim was to put the state on its feet, but in the form of a conservative and Catholic monarchy. For this purpose he made use of the Falange, placing himself at its head and turning it into a state party, but without giving it a central position of power. Franco also institutionalised the dictatorship, but less in a Fascist than in a monarchical, conservative direction, based on the clergy and high-ranking officers.

In Portugal, where in the 1920's not even 10 per cent of the population could read and write and similarly sharp contrasts existed as in Spain, one revolution followed another. Only these 10 per cent were entitled to vote. Heavy battles took place between the intellectuals. In 1926, after two unsuccessful military *putschs* and an abortive syndicalist revolt, General Carmona put an end to anarchic conditions by a *coup d'état* which had been prepared by the clergy. Carmona was at first both head of state and leader of the government, but later confined himself to the functions of head of state. The real ruler and dictator, Salazar, was appointed finance minister by Carmona in 1928 and then prime minister. Salazar was a professor of national economy and had not previously appeared in politics. He had taken no part in the *coup d'état* and when he appeared on the scene the dictatorial system was already installed. He quickly established his reputation as the highly competent and honest expert who succeeded in re-organising the ruined finances of Portugal and thereby the prostrate economy. He institutionalised the dictatorship by means of a constitution which gave the President the position of a constitutional monarch and through the founding of a single party with a militia and a youth organisation attached to which all young people between the ages of seven and twenty belonged. To this extent he made use of the Fascist pattern, but in a very moderate form. When Carmona died in 1951, a reliable supporter of Salazar became his successor.

Both in Spain and Portugal the dictatorships had arisen because of persistent functional disturbances in the state. To this extent they resembled the dictatorships of the one-time authoritarian zone. Both made use of ideological organisations to consolidate their power without allowing them paramount influence. Neither did they create any new type of state, but to a large extent preserved the old order, though adapting it—particularly in the case of Portugal—to modern conditions. Salazar and also Franco tried to create a corporate system, but in practice it functioned no better than in Austria and only had importance as a façade. In every respect the Austrian dictatorship had far fewer similarities with the Fascist dictatorship of Italy on which it leant for international reasons than with the Spanish and Portuguese. Different as Austrian social conditions were from those in Spain and Portugal, the three countries had various factors in common: the unbridgeable gulf between the political groups, the existence of strong extra-parliamentary forces and the concern of the Church for its position in the event of its opponents gaining the upper hand. None of the groups could maintain itself in power by parliamentary and democratic means and all therefore sought extra-parliamentary support. In all three countries, therefore, the clergy worked for a dictatorial régime and was one of its strongest props. Excluding Italy, one can therefore speak of Catholic dictatorships.

Finally, a brief word about Greece which had been in a perpetual state of war from 1912 to 1922 and since 1913 involved in repeated revolutionary turmoil. The monarchy was not able to survive for any length of time in face of its great opponent, the imperialist democratic republican Venizelos. But the republic proclaimed in 1924 could not master internal unrest, either. In 1925, General Pangalos carried out a military *putsch* and established an army dictatorship which was republican in colour, showed no particular ideological characteristics, but only lasted a year. King George II, who was restored in 1935, tried at first to rule through parliament, but in 1936, after a new and unsuccessful attempt at revolt by Venizelos against the republican opposition and the increasing activity of the Communists, the King appointed General Metaxas Prime Minister, furnishing him with full powers similar to those which Primo de Rivera had possessed in Spain. At that time, Metaxas very cautiously adopted some of the Fascist methods and forms, for instance the "Spartan" salute, but could find no support from a Fascist movement. This military dictatorship came to an end with the occupation of Greece.

Of the four unstable democracies in the West none was able to maintain a democratic form of government between the wars because it was inadequate for the functioning of the state. In all four states severe and persistent functional disturbances provoked the setting up of a dictatorship.

Thus, apart from Finland and Czechoslovakia whose democratic systems were destroyed by outside force, namely by Hitler, only those states were able to survive as democracies between the two world wars which had possessed a stable democratic form of government before the First World War.

ERNST FRAENKEL

Historical Handicaps of German Parliamentarism

Professor Ernst Fraenkel was born in 1898.
After becoming a Doctor of Law he practised
as a barrister in Berlin until 1938 when he
emigrated to the U.S.A. and entered public
service, working at first in Washington and
from 1946 to 1950 in Korea. Since 1953 he
has been Professor of Political Science at the
Free University of Berlin. His publications
include works on international law and the
American system of government.

Our constitutional thought lies under the trauma of the dissolution of the Weimar Republic. Outside Germany, too, the failed experiment of the first German republic is considered the classic example of an unsuccessful attempt to transfer uncritically the English parliamentary system of government to foreign countries without first examining whether the conditions necessary to its functioning are present. With the collapse of the Weimar Republic the naïve belief in the universal validity of this system seemed finally refuted. But both at home and abroad, people are perhaps inclined to stress the exemplary importance of the German tragedy between 1919 and 1933 while overlooking the fact that even before 30th January, 1933, all too many constitutions hastily erected after the English model had proved incapable of survival, for instance in Poland, Yugoslavia, Rumania and above all in Italy. But this raises the question whether the same process is going to be repeated after the Second World War. Unaffected by the experiences of the past, numerous states again proceeded after the Second World War to take over the parliamentary system of government as a recipe of perfection; less than fifteen years later, it became evident in Pakistan, Burma, Indonesia and, with certain reservations, also in France that these countries had obviously been attempting the impossible.

I do not intend to ask, let alone to answer here the anxious question whether this time Germany will prove immune to the immanent dangers to which the parliamentary system of government is always exposed when it is detached from its native English soil. The following remarks are confined to analysing the problem why in the past Germany has found it so difficult to understand the parliamentary system of government, to come to terms with it and to apply it successfully. The obstacles will be underlined which must be overcome before this most complicated and unstable of systems can function with the object of making a contribution to its permanent establishment in Germany. For one of the main sources of its frequent failure lies in the naïvety with which this—one might almost say—

27

chance product of English history is presented as a self-evident proposition, as a constitutional mechanism necessarily arising from the "nature of things"; similarly the attempt to detect constitutional principles of universal validity in a system which is only appropriate when it is based on certain pre-existing economic, sociological and ideological conditions is one reason for its frequent failure.

If any nation can be acquitted of underestimating the difficulties of transferring the parliamentary system to countries where it has not developed organically and automatically then it is the British themselves. The serious words may be remembered which were used by Lord Balfour in the Preface to Bagehot's *English Constitution* when he warned against copying British institutions without taking the peculiarities of the British temperament into account which had contributed so much to their successful functioning. "If it should transpire", he said prophetically in November, 1927, "that the borrowed constitution and the indigenous temperament are not properly suited to one another, then serious consequences might arise from the misshapen product."

Twenty years later, Ernest Barker took up the same problem and listed the conditions which helped to make possible the rise of the parliamentary system of government in England. He pointed to England's island position without, however, as all too often happens, giving this geopolitical circumstance an importance overshadowing all others; he stressed the relatively great flexibility of the English social structure which prevented any deep division ever arising between the aristocracy and the middle class; finally he underlined the importance of the inter-Protestant religious controversies for the intellectual and political climate of the English nation and explained that they took place between groups that were sufficiently united to agree on fundamentals and sufficiently disparate to be able to argue on matters of detail. But above all Barker stressed that certain psychological prerequisites are essential if the experiment of governing a country through parliament is to succeed. Barker believed that the parliamentary system of government had benefited from the basic attitude of empiricism which had prevailed in English political life and particularly from the typical English readiness to compromise and accept provisional solutions. Barker recommends that the urge to logic be confined to the study; for the arena of parliament he advises an attitude that should be primarily empirical without being specifically illogical.

The illusion, writes Barker, that the British constitution can be transferred at will to foreign countries springs from the false assumption that it is based on the abstract principle that parliament represents a nation composed of isolated individuals, whereas in fact it is based on the representation of group interests.

Just as the civil law in England is based on common law and precedent so constitutional law has developed to a great extent from conventions, parliamentary usage and rules of procedure which have become enshrined in the regulations for conducting business in the House of Commons.

Montesquieu's doctrine of the separation of powers offers a classic but by no means unique example of the European continental tendency to declare as principles of English constitutional law features which have developed organically during the course of centuries below the threshold of theoretical constitutional consciousness. Leopold von Ranke may have had this doctrine of the separation of powers in mind when he said that what appears to us as an idea is often merely an abstraction from some concrete phenomenon which is strange to us.

This may explain why exterior characteristics of English constitutional practice which do not fit into the hypostatised English constitutional system were ignored on the continent even when they were of vital importance for the functioning of a parliamentary régime. It has proved to be one of the most fateful handicaps of German parliamentarianism that it was conceived not as a facsimile of the English constitutional reality but according to the phantasm of a system of constitutional law foreign to the pragmatic English constitutional law. It is only in the recent past that an attempt has been made to correct this mistake.

With the aim of preventing a renewed failure of the parliamentary system of government the Basic Law has restricted the budgetary supremacy of the *Bundestag* and the *Bundesrat* and modified the vote of censure, thereby watering down the basic principles of what hitherto has been considered in Germany as the inalienable characteristic of parliamentarianism. According to Article 113 of the Basic Law parliament can only insert new items of expenditure or increase existing ones in the budgetary proposals laid before it if the Federal Government gives its approval; under Article 67 a vote of no confidence can only be passed on the Federal Chancellor if a majority of the *Bundestag* at the same time elects his successor.

Revolutionary though these provisions may seem to the European theoretician of parliamentarianism whose thought follows abstract and dogmatic paths, they, or at least their under-lying principles, are perfectly well known to the student of English constitutional practice.

The constitutional departures of the Basic Law from the Weimar constitution largely represent a closer approximation to the model of English parliamentarianism which in more than one respect was grossly misunderstood in 1919. Perhaps the most surprising feature of the new German "Chancellor democracy" is the amazement which the discovery of its existence has aroused.

The Chancellor democracy is a parallel phenomenon to the Prime Minister democracy with the most imporant condition that the Chancellor can only appeal to the people in the event of an open conflict with the parliamentary majority. In England, on the other hand, the Prime Minister possesses an unrestricted right of dissolution.

Not least the profound German misconceptions about the parliamentary system of government are due to the fact that it has been seen as the product of a uniform "Western democracy" without sufficiently differentiating between the characteristics which distinguish the English system of government which aims at the idea of representation and the plebiscitary characteristics which arose in the course of the French Revolution. This is not the place to discuss in detail how minds differed during the Revolution on the question whether the English representative system could be brought into harmony with the ideas of the French Revolution. It must suffice to recall that after the con-solidation of the constitution under the Bourbons and Louis Philippe English constitutional elements were fused with the basic principles of French constitutional thought and from this—as Georg Jellinek pointed out more than half a century ago—the specific form of continental parliamentarianism arose: "Con-tinental parliamentarianism is not so much of English as of French origin and the prevailing parliamentary theory was worked out at the time of the Restoration and the July Monarchy."

Parliamentary thought on the continent of Europe, including

the German, rests on a rejection of the idea that parliament is the place where the pluralistic forces of society strive to balance one another. With few exceptions the German parliaments did not develop organically out of the social classes, but were designed and set up as an abstract counterweight to the class structure. Jellinek has called modern parliaments outside England "institutions without a history" and said of them that "in the whole of the past there is hardly another example of an organisation so suddenly created and intended to change the state completely". Members of parliament were called on to abandon the thought that they represented particular interests; rather they were to act as though they were spokesmen solely for the general welfare. After parliament had been accorded the position of one of the highest organs of state it was judged in Germany by standards applicable to some hypothetical "realm of freedom" but not to a state ruled by "reason and necessity".

Detached from its social basis which necessarily had to be a pluralistic one such a parliament saw itself transported to a spirit world in which it was condemned either to sterility or to break out into social reality. Suffering under the obsessional neurosis of being exclusively the exponent of a largely fictitious general will, in taking care of the interests of his constituents the individual member of parliament acted with a bad conscience. As long as he was unable to claim openly the double role of a representative of the nation and the mouthpiece of particular interests he was obliged to disguise his championship of special interests under the halo of protecting communal needs. But thereby the frank settlement of conflicts between group interests which necessarily arise in every pluralistic society had to be undertaken with the false pathos of a basic discussion of universal principles, thus poisoning the atmosphere of parliament and undermining the realism of its proceedings. In the ambivalent attitude of German parliaments towards the social basis of their own existence the popular instinct detected a lack of honesty and was inclined to accuse parliament and its members of ideological self-deception, if not of a deliberate attempt to deceive the people. This explains the attempt to make a clean and clear distinction between the representation of the general welfare and of particular interests.

Thus it would almost seem as though the parliamentary representation of special interests was not the main cause of objection so much as its disguise under ideological trimmings. One of the characteristics of the traditional German disgust with parliament lies in the fact that it was repeatedly allied to a call for a revival of the corporate state on the part of people who at the same time were usually inclined to authoritarian tenden- cies. Inner resistance to parliament as one of the highest organs of state will not be overcome so long as the dogma is upheld that the common weal possesses a pre-established grandeur of its own and the view is dogmatically rejected that the common weal is represented by the end result arising from the parallelogram of the economic, social, political and ideological forces of a nation whenever a balance is aimed at and achieved which objectively corresponds to the minimum requirements of a just social order and subjectively is not felt by any important group to disregard its interests.

In 1946, no less a man than Winston Churchill openly admitted of himself and his parliamentary colleagues that they represented interests and possessed group connections. To main- tain the contrary, he said, would be ridiculous and could be expected at the best in heaven, but fortunately not in the British parliament.

Now we have heard *ad nauseam* in the course of the last thirty years that the justification of parliament from the point of view of intellectual history lies in free discussion between deputies who are tied neither to interests nor party groups and who in the course of this discussion are in a position to discover the truth, here synonymous with the common good.

A political phenomenon like parliamentarianism cannot be explained exclusively by the methods of intellectual history with- out taking sufficiently into account its social and economic basis. But if a sociological supplements an ideological analysis of the classical period of French parliamentarianism—so admired by Carl Schmitt—during the July Monarchy, it becomes plain that in France in the age of Guizot (who was a contemporary of Balzac) a form of parliamentarianism prevailed under the operation of the suffrage according to income in which bribery of the electorate, patronage and corruption of individual deputies—in short, the practice of what English parliamentary history euphemistically calls "influence"—was not only a daily occurrence, but was considered essential for the formation of parliamentary majorities. With few exceptions, "influence"

ERNST FRAENKEL 33

played and still plays a decisive role in countries which are in a condition of ambivalent legitimacy, that is to say are under the rule of a regime for which Guglielmo Ferrero has derived from Louis Philippe the name "Philippism".

The one great country in which Philippism has never found a foothold is Germany. Large-scale parliamentary debates where the victory or defeat of a government is sealed in open battle are no part of the German tradition. The flexible parliamentary tactics of independent-minded deputies are also unknown in Germany. In Germany there is no parliamentary style which has developed from the feeling of solidarity between the members of the different parties or cliques who assure one another with winks and smiles that they "know the form" and have no intention of infringing the rules of parliamentary solidarity. German parliamentary style has been formed neither by cynical aristocrats of the *ancien régime* nor by hypocritical bourgeois preaching the *juste milieu* who understood how to apply the rules of parliamentary procedure in an elegant fashion because they had a feeling for the playful element in the interaction of parliamentary forces. German parliamentary style has been developed by honourable men to whose seriousness of purpose based on fidelity to principles the idea of a political game would have appeared frivolous. Germany skipped the period of parliamentarianism in which parliamentary decisions depended on the co-operation and counterplay of cliques possessing patronage. Germany has no memory of parliaments in which it was relatively simple to form working majorities because the force which kept majorities together was their participation in the power of government, in other words the fact that the supporters of the government were "in".

German parliamentarianism escaped the period of party patronage because Germany possessed a trained, organised and incorruptible bureaucracy with appointment for life and a unique system of professional protection for its employees before ever parliaments were founded. No comparative analysis of the structure of the German and English systems of parliamentary government should overlook the fact that behind the outward similarity of the two systems lies a fundamental difference which springs not least from the different order in which bureaucracy and parliament arose in the two countries. In England the parliamentary system was developed in the seventeenth and

eighteenth centuries and the civil service was built into it in the
nineteenth century; in Germany a bureaucratic system was
developed in the seventeenth and eighteenth centuries which
was capped by a parliament in the nineteenth century. It is
certainly one of the titles to fame of the German bureaucratic
state that under its sway the formation of parties dispensing
patronage and the triumph of "influence" never came about; but
it was also to the detriment of the German parliamentary state
that in its years of apprenticeship it was unable to prove its
worth with a party system more suitable than any other for
the conclusion of compromises, the adoption of provisional
solutions and the avoidance of argument on matters of
principle.

Since the early days of parliamentarianism in Germany a
uniquely well developed bureaucracy had barred the way to the
executive for parliament, its members and parties and had
managed, citing Montesquieu's principle of the separation of
powers, to confine them almost exclusively to the sphere of
legislation. But under legislation was meant by definition the
setting of universally valid norms.

Anchored to the thesis that the "general will" was already in
existence and robbed of a chance to test the practicability of the
abstractly formulated principles of their legislative programmes,
the German parties were bound to sink into a doctrinairism
which today still weighs uncomfortably on the German parliamentary system.

In addition, the existence of a multi-party system was
closely connected with the fact that parliament had nothing
to do with questions of patronage and was almost exclusively
occupied with the discussion of legislative matters. By insisting
that such questions were removed from the competence of
parliament the German bureaucracy contributed to the formation of parties in circumstances which made compromise difficult
and the formation of parliamentary majorities impossible. The
German multi-party system and the predominant role of the
bureaucracy were complementary phenomena in Imperial
Germany.

But the attempt by the bureaucratic state to banish
parliament to the sphere of abstract principle was not only due
to the understandable desire of officialdom not to become the
plaything of parliamentary cliques; it also sprang from the civil

servants' wish to remove their performance in office from parliamentary control.

The rules of procedure in the Imperial Reichstag not only made it impossible for parliament to check how the abstract norms in the laws it had helped to frame were applied, they also prevented parliament from acquiring the factual information which it needed in order to form an independent opinion of the economic and social implications of the bills it was to discuss.

The German parliaments put up hardly any defence against the attempt of the government to cut them off from contact with outsiders. Did they feel instinctively that the more intensively they busied themselves with the empirical basis of proposed legislation, the greater care they took through the examination of witnesses and experts to acquaint themselves with the facts connected with it, the more obvious it became that their claim to represent an alleged "general will" was an empty dream? Did it dawn on them that parties which are obliged to concern themselves with the empiricism of politics cannot pass over or conceal the pluralistic character of society? Did they come to realise that though an enforced concentration on the empiricism of politics entails the abandonment of programmes based on principle it also opens up the prospect of understanding that, far from being objectionable by definition, compromise is the salt of politics?

In the long run, the idea of the parliamentary system will only be fully accepted in Germany when the concept of the people has been successfully demythologised and the concept of the state demystified. The power of the English parliament was first tested in the struggle against the metaphysic of the state which James I used as an ideological smoke-screen. A parliamentary system of government cannot flourish in an atmosphere fraught with myth and the cult of mysteries. Among the handicaps of German parliamentarianism was the chain reaction which arose through the fact that the mystification of the state helped to create the myth of the class war and the myth of the class war contributed to mythologise the "folk community".

This may be the explanation of why wide sections of the German nation have declined to see themselves represented in any other dress than the fairy costume of a completely homogeneous people. To them this was the only possible way of repressing their unease at the small degree of cohesion which Germany had achieved in political reality. They hated the sight of a parliament split into parties and groups representing diverse interests, not because they saw in it a caricature, but a true picture of their own life which they felt it essential to idealise.

In the work of his old age on *Popular Government* written towards the end of the Victorian period the great historian of English law, Sir Henry Maine, raised the question whether a form of parliamentary corruption might not arise in an era of mass party organisations which would have even more dangerous effects than the bribery of the old régime.

A dogmatic *laissez-faire* liberalism in Henry Maine's sense has hardly ever existed in Germany and that may explain why the German parties were able to devote themselves so early and so intensively to becoming the spokesmen of the collective interests of large industrial associations. German parliamentarianism suffered the further handicap that the parties increasingly became the agents of these associations in so far as their practical interests were concerned, but without sacrificing their dogmatic attitude to internal and external political questions as a whole, so that ideologically these large associations became dependent on the parties. The symbiosis of parties and groups—from which the "integral party" arose—which was characteristic of the development of Imperial Germany and the Weimar Republic meant that Bismarck achieved his short-term aim of reducing the numbers of parties, but that his long-term aim of removing ideology from politics failed. On the contrary, it brought ideological tensions to group battles even outside parliament. When the struggle for a few pfennigs' unemployment insurance involves questions of faith, then parliamentarianism is bound to collapse.

Since the days of Aristotle it has been repeatedly asserted that the best constitution for a state is a mixed constitution. It is appropriate to ask whether for a party, too, the best constitution is not one in which the various structural elements are "properly" mixed : the personalities, the economic and social elements and the ideological.

It has become a commonplace today which is recognised even in the Basic Law that parties are essential if the German parliamentary system of government is to function. They help to form the popular will by concentrating the numerous pluralistic groups of the people into a small number of political blocks for the specific purpose of forming parliamentary majorities, but without endangering their existence or function; they help to form the will of the state by subjecting the elected representatives of the people to a strict party discipline without which the individual deputy would be hopelessly at the mercy of those interests on whose support he depends for his re-election.

Our difficulty does not lie in realising that parties are indispensible for the functioning of parliamentary government; our difficulty consists in the fact that in order to function a system of parliamentary government requires a different type of party than the ones which have been thrown up in the course of German history: parties which are not ashamed to admit that it is their aim to lift their leaders into the strategically important positions in the government and administration; parties which are not ashamed to admit that they must work hand in hand with group interests without capitulating to the groups; parties which are not ashamed to admit that they exert pressure on their members because without party discipline parliamentary government is impossible. We need parties which possess the inner strength to cut free from traditional conceptions because they arose in different political circumstances and represent merely a dead weight on the functioning of parliament. But we also need parties which, while admitting the need for a pragmatic attitude to politics, are not ashamed to confess some residue of romantic attachment to the dreams of their youth when everything was so fine in politics because we really believed that principles ruled the world.

The disintegration of the Weimar Republic which I mentioned at the beginning of this talk was an historical event which certainly cannot be ascribed to any one cause. International and economic factors played at least as great a part as the structural defects which appeared in that system of government. But this should not mislead us into overlooking the fact that the paralysis of parliament which precipitated the collapse of the Weimar Republic sprang not least from the failure of the political parties which proved incapable of fulfilling the functions which devolve upon them in a constitutional pluralistic parliamentary democracy.

KURT SONTHEIMER

Anti-democratic Thought in the Weimar Republic

Professor Kurt Sontheimer was born in 1928. From 1949 to 1953 he studied sociology and history at the universities of Freiburg, Kansas (U.S.A.) and Erlangen and from 1953 to 1954 at the Institut d'Etudes Politiques in Paris. From 1957 to 1960 he worked on a research project for the Institute of Contemporary History in Munich on anti-democratic ideas in the Weimar Republic. He published a book on this subject in 1962. Since 1962 he has been Professor of Political Science at the Free University of Berlin.

In an essay which Ernst Jünger wrote before the collapse of the Weimar Republic there is a noteworthy reference to the historian whose task it might one day be to explore political ideas in Germany after the First World War. We read:

"The future historian of these post-war years which one hopes he will be able to call the years of the German revolution will not find it easy to display their stock of ideas as clearly as an exact historical portrayal requires. But certainly he will not find that lack of ideas of which this period is sometimes accused today —on the contrary, even in the craziest moments of its rule the Convention did not equal the present variety and complexity of endeavours. It seems rather that in a state of disturbance life is least able to offer resistance to ideas, that it succumbs to a kind of overfertilisation, a heated battle of unborn conditions which are struggling to become reality."

At that time Ernst Jünger himself took part in the efforts of not a few German intellectuals to give Germany, which had emerged from the First World War as a defeated nation, an intellectual and political renewal and to bring about the long overdue revolution. Twenty to thirty years after the remarks we have quoted were written, historians are in fact in process of sorting the ideas, as Jünger said, or of inquiring to what extent the fate of the Weimar Republic is mirrored in the political ideas of that time.

Strive as we may for the cool and dispassionate objectivity of the historian, we still cannot look at the history of the Weimar Republic without taking in the twelve-year period of German and European history which followed. The fourteen years of Weimar are overshadowed by the twelve years of Hitler's dictatorship—and consciously or unconsciously almost all discussions about the Weimar Republic start with the question: how was it possible?

At a very early stage, scientific historians isolated and examined some of the essential factors which led to the fateful collapse of the Weimar Republic. The search still continues. The historical judgement required in answer to this question—which is still important for our present political consciousness—must necessarily be complex and differentiated. Generalised answers are no longer adequate. It was neither the world economic crisis, nor the post-war policy of the "Entente Powers", nor alone the failure of the political parties, nor the questionable attitude of President Hindenburg in the months preceding Hitler's eleva-tion to the Chancellorship which dealt the death blow to the Republic. Neither would the structural weaknesses of the Republic have been sufficient on their own to make its collapse inevitable if they had not coincided with fateful political decisions made by individuals. But again these were only so serious because they paved the way for Hitler's dictatorship, though it was hardly possible to foresee in 1933 that ten years later he would cast away Germany's unseasonably predominant position in a fit of blind rage.

Great historical breaks almost always result from a combina-tion of circumstances, personal decisions and structural condi-tions, but this combination has seldom grown to such complexity as in the stages of the collapse of the Weimar Republic. The multiplicity of factors which led Germany into Hitler's dictator-ship still therefore makes it difficult for the historian to supply a synopsis or a picture of all the phenomena involved. Moreover we are still not out of the stage which must precede any rounded historical judgement, the stage of detailed investigation which starts at chosen points in order to assess the part played by various forces, persons and structural factors. Here I am going to discuss one particular aspect of the whole problem, namely the nature of anti-democratic thought in the Weimar Republic.

It is hardly a matter of controversy today that certain ideological predispositions in German thought generally, but particularly in the intellectual and political climate of the Weimar Republic, induced a large number of German electors under the Weimar Republic to consider the National Socialist movement as less problematic than it in fact turned out to be. There is also little doubt that the Weimar Republic lacked internal support, in other words, the Republic was not looked on by many people as a state in which they desired to live or to which they were prepared to give positive encouragement. The political ideolo-gies and aspirations of the Weimar period can be looked at from two points of view: in reference to National Socialist thought and in regard to their function within the framework of the

Republic itself. Both methods of approach have already been explored. While the Nazis were still in power, some foreign historians—the best known among them being the French expert on German history Edmond Vermeil—searched German intellectual histoiry for antecedents of National Socialist thought, going back in some cases as far as Martin Luther. Though some analogies can be drawn between National Socialist thought and certain ideas of earlier decades and centuries, this procedure is largely unhistorical and unsuited to the true situation. It overlooks the fact that, despite its assertion to the contrary, National Socialism possessed no compact ideological system of its own but manipulated ideas for its own purposes as it required them and it raises the purely outward identity of National Socialist thoughts with the statements of previous epochs to the level of formal proof, whereas in every case the historical context of these statements would have to be examined. There is some reason for claiming that by such methods it would not be difficult to find antecedents of National Socialist thought in the literature of Western countries.

But except for the American Shirer who appears to have had a "relapse", this procedure is hardly used today. Instead, there is a plethora of short studies and more ambitious projects which examine the political pronouncements of individuals and groups in the Weimar and the preceding Imperial period. Though this method does not clarify the Nazi ideology, it does throw light on the intellectual atmosphere in which, when National Socialism arose, it could seem to be a more or less presentable doctrine. National Socialism, moreover, derived considerable profit from thinkers like Oswald Spengler, Moeller van den Bruck and Ernst Jünger, despite the fact that later it emphatically rejected them. But here, too, it is difficult to confine the problem to a greater or lesser degree of conformity with National Socialist thought as a whole because there is no strict canon of National Socialist thought which could make conformity significant. For that reason the unsystematic, unco-ordinated character of the National Socialist ideology has frequently been stressed and the reproach made that it represents a conglomerate of ideas. All the same, it was this very lack of ideological fixation which in the last years of the Weimar Republic made National Socialism a refuge for those many people who hoped that it would improve conditions in the way they wanted. Its ideological fluidity, what an author once called the "porridge of ideas", was indeed an essential condition for the political success of the Nazis.

For these reasons it seems more meaningful for historical research in the field of political thought to examine the role played by this thought with reference to the Republic itself. Anti-democratic thought is not thereby equated with National Socialist thought, for its aim was simply to replace the Weimar Republic with other forms of political control. By intellectually undermining the existing state and campaigning for an alternative in whatever form it brought about a kind of intellectual consumption of democracy and prevented opinion giving it that wide degree of support which is essential to a democratic constitution if it is to function at all.

Democracy is familiar with the principle of opposition and approves it, but opposition does not mean resistance to the state and its basic constitutional principles, but opposition to a certain policy within the framework of the same principles approved by all. But opposition in the Weimar Republic was to a great extent opposition to the Republic and to democracy as such. In this respect it was anti-democratic. The historian, therefore, who concerns himself with anti-democratic thought in the Weimar Republic has to deal with the ideas and critical thought of those individuals and groups who were opposed to the Weimar Republic and wished to see it abolished. It is obvious that this thought played a part in the National Socialist seizure of power because it helped through its tendency against the existing state to clear the ground in which a big oppositional movement like the mass National Socialist party could unfold. But we would catch only a glimpse of the important role falling to this anti-democratic attitude in the process of democratic decline during the Weimar period if we started by identifying it, as so many people are inclined to do, with National Socialism.

An example will make this clear. In 1932, the well-known publicist and politician Ernst Niekisch, the leading man in the so-called "national Bolshevist" school during the Weimar period, published a small book entitled *Hitler—a German Fatality*. The title seems to justify the book, for Hitler became indeed a disaster for Germany. And in his forceful warning against the demagogue Hitler Niekisch saw many things correctly. Nevertheless, in essence Niekisch's book is more the product of a misguided utopian than of a democrat seeking to defend the Weimar

Republic. Niekisch's main charge against Hitler is that he would
lead the German people yet deeper into the slavery of the
Versailles system instead of freeing them by turning to Russia.
Niekisch no less than Hitler was bent on destroying the Weimar
Republic. By founding a so-called "resistance group" he did
manage to keep his few supporters clear of the Nazi Party, but
there was nothing in the national Bolshevist programme of this
group to induce any of its members to raise a finger to protect
the Republic from the Nazi threat. To have been against Hitler,
therefore, does not in any way mean to have fought for the con-
tinuance of the Weimar Republic.

Thus "anti-democratic thought" is merely a general term
covering the wide variety of intellectual tendencies which
developed during the fourteen years of the Republic and, taken
together, left the Weimar democracy without adequate support
from the educated classes. Though differing from one another,
they all saw the existing Republic as an enemy and not as an
object of loyalty and therefore their final effect on the Weimar
Republic was destructive.

But many of those people who for the time being had no
means of realising their aspirations and expressed their discontent with the existing form of government through anti-
democratic tracts and pamphlets finally gave their support to
the National Socialist mass movement. In many cases they did
not do this because they sympathised entirely with the ideas of
the movement, but because they saw in Hitler's party the growth
of a political force which they confidently hoped would bring
the tottering Weimar democracy to its fall. Thus on the one
hand anti-democratic thought brought about a situation in
which, despite divergences of political opinion, a large number
of its adherents finally opted for Hitler and on the other hand it
also had a destructive effect on the Republic whenever a direct
conflict arose between the anti-democratic group and the Hitler
movement. Its historical significance for the Republic as well as
for what followed only becomes fully apparent when both these
aspects are borne in mind.

One must agree with Ernst Jünger whom I quoted at the start
of this talk that it is not easy to sort and arrange the mass of
anti-democratic ideas. The points of view and the intellectual
positions they express extend over a very large scale, it being

possible, after all, to become an opponent of a weak democratic republic for the widest number of reasons. According to our definition of anti-democratic, Communist thought of course is also anti-democratic—and as everyone knows both Communists and National Socialists played a part in making the Weimar Republic incapable of manoeuvre despite the fact that they were sworn enemies and did their best to murder one another in street battles.

But in the following survey of the essential content of the anti-democratic movement in the Weimar period we will confine ourselves to the anti-democratic thought of the right-wing nationalists. Apart from the national Bolshevist variants of those times, the Communist line of thought is clear enough : to the Communist the Weimar Republic was a bourgeois republic in which the working class was oppressed and exploited by the capitalist middle class. The way to pure democracy in the Communist sense entails the dictatorship of the proletariat which seeks the realisation of a Socialist society under leadership of the Communist Party by means of revolution or the application of evolutionary tactics.

The anti-democratic thought of the right-wing nationalists, on the other hand, was richer and more differentiated. It ranged from deep speculation on the philosophy of politics down to the primitive antisemitic pamphlet. The broad effect which it exerted on the intellectual life of the Weimar Republic would have been inconceivable without the intellectual and cultural upheaval which took place in every sphere of life at the beginning of the twentieth century.

The intellectual upheaval at the start of the century which reached its peak in the 1920's was certainly not confined to Germany alone, but it achieved its maximum effect in that country. It can be generally defined as a counter-movement against the bourgeois world based on the ideas of the French Revolution and of liberalism and against its political, economic and social forms. The new thought found its philosophical expression in the discovery of the fluid, incalculable and irrational element in all aspects of life and thus became opposed to philosophical rationalism and the modern scientific movement initiated by Descartes. Artistically this attitude to life and the intellect was conveyed in the Expressionistic *Lebensschrei*, politically and

economically in increasing opposition to the political and economic forms of liberalism, that is to say, to democratic parliamentarianism and capitalism.

Irrationalism was a basic characteristic in right-wing anti-
democratic thought. But though the "philosophy of life" in its
somewhat pretentious clothing represented a genuine and meaningful reaction to the excessive stress placed on rationalism in the
second half of the nineteenth century and to the incipient mass
technicalisation of life as a whole, the widespread popularisation
and the accompanying abasement of this line of thought made
the pendulum swing much too far. Irrationalism became not
merely a necessary corrective to rationalism in its more arid and
life-destroying forms, it developed into a fashionable obsession
which denied the right of any other type of thought to exist.
Condensed into a set of formulae, Ludwig Klages' large-scale
polemical examination of the "Mind as Enemy of the Soul" became the creed of many German intellectuals who in that capacity found nothing better to do than to mock the intellect as
cold and hostile to life and by exalting life as such, the instincts,
the blood, pure vitality and the attachment of human beings to
"Mother Earth" turned themselves into "thinkers" who despised
thought.

All this might not have been so serious if irrationalism had
stayed in the field of philosophy, but as the new feeling of life,
as manifested for instance in the youth movement as a protest
against the bourgeois society of Imperial Germany, was often
allied to a hectic thirst for action and was in no way satisfied
with exercises in contemplation, this popular stream of thought
finally became the forcing ground for social utopias. After the
ideas of the nineteenth century symbolised by the word "liberalism" had been declared fit for the scrap-heap, these were then
producd as representing the leading ideas of the twentieth
century. This combination of irrationalism with a feeling of
vitality and an urge to political action marked the birth of anti-
democratic thought such as prevailed under the Weimar
Republic.

Of course, this thought possessed many points of contact with
our intellectual history, in particular with the ideas of Romanticism which in its turn had been a reaction against the extremes
of the age of enlightenment and its intellectual tendencies. But
a hundred years later, the effect of the clash was incomparably

more dynamic and destructive. The new ideas were now directed against a highly planned and technicalised environment, against a mass civilisation which yet could not be averted, against the tendency inherent in the modern industrial age towards a progressive rationalisation of life, and against the process which Max Weber had called the law of the age and which robbed the world of its magic. The result was, to use an expression of Thomas Mann's, a kind of technicalised romanticism. The questionable element in this intellectual development was not the discovery of the importance of myth and symbolism in literature and art, not the ecstatic interest shown in primeval times or in the customs of other civilisations such as the Asiatic, but the infusion of political ideas with elements from these spheres. In its legitimate form Thomas Mann by no means rejected the new irrationalism, but he thought there was hardly anything more terrible than its popularisation and this and its application to politics he called the "botching of the philosophy of life".

The adoration of life, indeed, was equivalent to rejecting the critical function of the intellect. Human beings, said the popular philosophers of the hour—Oswald Spengler, Friedrich Georg Jünger, Paul Krannhals and others—should not make their decisions with bloodless reason, but with the strength of their heart and blood. They should cease vegetating in artificial communities which appointed governments by mechanical elections, but gather in a natural community as a people and choose a leader who would guide them to a better future. In short, in politics the basic axioms of the *Lebensphilosophie* were directed against parliamentary democracy and the so-called democratic system. On the new intellectual basis other conceptions of the state were evolved which would leave the mechanical democratic state with its party rule and its irresponsible anonymity behind and bring new and greater forces into play.

The "true" state, for example, which the influential sociologist Othmar Spann proclaimed, was to be an organic, that is to say a hierarchic state; formal democracy was to be replaced by "folkic" democracy, the mechanism of social life to be transformed by the creation of new communal institutions, the anonymous rule of the civil service dissolved in favour of personal responsibility exercised by charismatic leaders, the "asphalt civilisation" of the towns superseded by human settlements rooted to the soil, civilisation itself outshone by the blossoming of a genuine folkic culture.

All these antitheses reveal that the new political vocabulary sprang from the popularised *Lebensphilosophie* of the 1920's. The sociologist Helmuth Plessner has described how the level of this philosophy became lowered thereby enabling irrationalism to enter politics in the following words: "The fruit of *Lebensphilosophie* had to ripen one day. Every great thought which seizes hold of the masses shapes their expectations and grows through these into deeds. It loses its depth and subtlety, its uncertainties and its equivocations, its frankness and plasticity. But even in this coarse form imposed on it by the needs of mass propaganda it still retains its connection with its intellectual and ideological origins."

Anti-democratic thought resulted from a polemical attitude. It aimed to kill liberal democracy and its first target was therefore democratic institutions and the spirit behind them. In this way it succeeded in making many Germans disgusted with the democratic republic. In the background of these polemics hovered a new and different form of state which was propagated in many variants—the authoritarian or totalitarian state, the corporate state, the German people's state, the folkic community. The most comprehensive formula used to combat the Weimar Republic and its constitution was the assertion that this state was the product of western political thought. But western democracy, it was said, could never be a suitable form of government for Germany, the "middle country", and it was up to the Germans to devise their own form, to renounce "rotten Westernism" as it was contemptuously called and to create a self-supporting political structure out of the strength of the German nation, the springs of German blood and the particular circumstances of Germany's situation. An imitation of western democracy and its liberalism meant nothing less than the progressive decline of Germany, the abandonment of the idea of the *Reich* as the form of state most suited to it, the betrayal of *Kultur* to civilisation. In positively savage articles Spengler propounded the opinion that every country must find its own political structure—nothing was therefore more foolish than to imitate foreign models. England, he said, knew well enough why it recommended its parliamentarianism to foreign countries, because it acted on them like poison.

The critical attitude to western thought was expressed in other polemical concepts. To western democratism was opposed the idea of a German folkic community, to the idea of equality the demand for a graded hierarchical organisation, to individualism universalism. Othmar Spann for instance, saw the whole of world history caught in the ineluctable polarity of individualism and universalism. He pleaded for universalism, saw individualism as pure destruction and held out as the means of salvation from anarchy and the complete atomisation of society the corporate state which was not democratic because it condemned the principle of equality. Other people preferred the antithesis between individualism and Socialism. But the Socialism of this type was not identical with the international Socialism of Karl Marx's school which was included with liberal thought, but was a Socialism of the community. The idea of the community contained in it was also a fashionable concept of that time and derived its polemical content from the antithesis to society. Though the sociologist Ferdinand Toennies in his famous book on "Community and Society" called the "community" a thing of the past, the mushrooming ideologists of the community idea wanted to turn mass society back into organic communities, depopulate the towns and make the rural and federal forms of community life the sole guiding principle in politics. The idea of a German or national Socialism was in the last resort synonymous with the idea of the folkic community which was the final goal of the movement for renewal. The anti-democrats, too, found it necessary to think in folkic terms. But to many people this was equivalent to thinking as a German and to them "German" meant first and foremost the non-Jewish element, so that in many groups and circles the idea of the "folk community" congealed into a primitive anti-semitic ideology which in this barbaric form also dominated National Socialism.

When these polemical concepts were combined with the vocabulary of the *Lebensphilosophie* an extraordinarily suggestive effect emerged. The popular *Lebensphilosophie* used words like "cold", "stiff", "dead" in contrast to "living", "organic", "flourishing". The politicised "philosophy of life" then applied such adjectives to the political and social phenomena of the time. The democratic form of government was called "mechanical" or "mechanistic" because it rested on the principle of free and equal elections carried out mechanically; parliament passed as a voting machine without any real relation to the people; the government was a largely anonymous and irresponsible apparatus for exercising rule—the whole so-called "system" was dubbed "stiff", "inorganic" and "mechanistic". The people who lived under it were split up into individualistic atoms without any point of contact with an overriding whole or any participation in a community filled by a uniform will.

This was how the anti-democratic ideologists saw their environment and they did not hesitate to label all the phenomena which they hated as "hostile to life", "stiff", "mechanistic", etc., while they associated their own political utopias with the idea of life. The antithesis was somewhat unfair, for *a priori*, of course, life is more attractive than death and stagnation, what is organic arouses more sympathy than the purely mechanical and creative quality—which the ideologists claimed to possess—held greater promise than mere quantity.

It was this mixture of *Lebensphilosophie* and political ideology which made the existing form of government seem so contemptible, valueless and inappropriate, while it decked its own however unrealistic conceptions of the state with the glamour of perfection. But if, as Spengler once said, life was the alpha and omega and mere vitality and strength were the measure of its fullness and value, then the final consequence—which became a grim reality under National Socialism—was the destruction in the name of the people of all life considered unworthy to be alive.

So far we have dealt very summarily with some of the central ideas and concepts of anti-democratic thought. Undoubtedly its most effective polemic referred to the political institutions set up under the Weimar Republic. The most constant and rewarding target of anti-democratic criticism was parliamentarianism and the party system. The conviction was widespread that the parliamentary system was due to expire, being no longer a democratic form of government suitable to the twentieth century. In a very effective analysis of the political situation Carl Schmitt showed that modern parliamentarianism had lost its intellectual basis and he pleaded, followed by many others, for a total democracy in which liberal principles would have no place. "Democracy" and "dictatorship" now suddenly appeared, not as conflicting, but as perfectly reconcilable concepts because it might be the will of the people to have a dictator by acclamation. The folkic state of the Third Reich with its *Führer* was thus completely in accord with these ideas which were labelled as genuinely democratic.

Contempt was also poured on the parties of the Weimar Republic and on the party system as such. Certainly this system had its inordinate weaknesses in the Weimar period, but the polemic against the parties was so subjectively emotional that in extreme cases it portrayed them as positively harmful to the people, as foreign bodies which only served their private interests while neglecting the interests of the whole. Spengler spoke cynically of the Weimar Republic as a "firm". In its constitution, he said, there was no mention of the people, but only of parties, no talk of power, honour or greatness, but only of parties; there was no goal and no future for Germany, but only the interests of parties. In five years, German parliamentarianism had produced no ideas and no decisions, not even an attitude.

What difference did it make that in the Weimar constitution the function of parties in helping to form a political will was unfortunately not referred to, although Spengler asserted the contrary—the parties as the organisations engaged in the battle for political power were among the best hated institutions in the Republic. With good reason Hitler insisted on the idea of the "National Socialist movement" in contrast to a political party like others and not a few Germans were convinced that in supporting the NSDAP (National Socialist German Workers' Party) they were joining a political movement which was not like other parties, particularly as it had given the promise—which it promptly fulfilled—that it would abolish the nuisance of parties in Germany as soon as it came to power.

All the same, the Weimar Republic needed the consensus of the parties to achieve anything in the political field and from the start it was a misfortune that some of the parties represented in parliament did not support the democratic republic, but were themselves anti-democratic in their aims. This applied to the parties on the extreme right and left, but also to the German Nationalists and to some extent to the German People's Party and other splinter parties.

Surveying anti-democratic ideas in the Weimar Republic and

disregarding the anti-democratic activity of the Left, we can distinguish two main tendencies : an old and a new nationalism. The old nationalism centred politically in the German Nationalists, the former Conservatives, who in the Weimar Republic aimed at a restoration, not to say reaction. Their political impulse sprang from memories of Germany's splendour under Kaiser Wilhelm and the great age of Bismarck. On the other hand, the new nationalism with its numerous ramifications was not much interested in a restoration of the monarchy, but agreed with the youth movement in finding Wilhelmism stale and unprofitable and hoped to supersede it by revolutionary means. Although the Weimar Republic had brought about considerable social and political changes, the young nationalists looked on it as an unwarrantable continuation of the old régime and worked with all their strength for an intellectual and political revolution in Germany. Among them anti-democratic thought found its most nourishing soil and there were hundreds of different groups of varying tendencies—National Revolutionaries, National Bolshevists, Young Conservatives or Young Nationalists—who sought to overthrow or reform the Weimar structure. The new nationalism received a strong impulse from the so-called "war experience" which on the one hand explains the harsh, militant vocabulary of its pronouncements and on the other was considered the model on which the new folk community and its heroic conception of life would be based. The young anti-democratic right-wingers wanted to forge a community of warriors out of a liberal-minded people of shop-keepers and according to Ernst Jünger's famous book on the "Worker" the middle-class citizens were to be turned into soldiers and workers.

There is no doubt that, shaped by such authors as Wilhelm Stapel, Oswald Spengler, Arthur Moeller van den Bruck, Ernst and Friedrich Georg Jünger, Ernst Niekisch, August Winnig and many others, the thought of the young right-wing nationalists prepared the intellectual soil for the growth of National Socialism. The Conservative Revolution which they wanted to bring about was exploited by the mass movement of National Socialism, particularly as the new nationalism had no effective political representation—in contrast to the old nationalism which had its home in Hugenberg's *Deutschnationale Volkspartei*. The paradoxical combination of the idea of preservation and overthrow underlying the Conservative Revolution was deliberate, for through the revolutionary renewal of the German people and their system of government a conservative system of values, alleged to be eternal, was to be restored. A Conservative Revolution therefore meant a revolution for the preservation of endangered conservative values. The new state which it was desired to bring about was to be based once more on the bedrock of the people's life, it was to preserve the German soul in its pristine form and protect it from exploitation by foreign institutions and unscrupulous party demagogues. The conservative revolutionaries thought there was hardly anything worth preserving in the Weimar democracy.

The revolution came—in the form of National Socialism. Not all those who had hoped for an upheaval and had loaded their pens with pathos and aggression in the battle against Weimar were in agreement with the National Socialist form of the German folkic state which then came about and few found their dreams fulfilled of a perfect *Reich der Deutschen*. Indeed some of the conservative revolutionaries became outspoken opponents of the régime and paid for their opposition with death. But though the fact was not admitted, as a political mass movement National Socialism had been able to profit from the hostility to the Republic generated by the anti-democratic intellectuals and derived great strength from it.

When we are confronted today with the essays, pamphlets and articles written against the Weimar Republic in the years of its existence much of their content strikes us as incomprehensible and deluded. But a closer look at the intellectual atmosphere then prevailing in politics shows that anti-democratic ideas were widespread. The subjection of a large part of intellectual Germany to the National Socialist *Weltanschauung*, later raised to the status of a religion, could hardly have taken place without the anti-democratic movement which preceded it. In its contempt for everything liberal it had blunted people's minds to the inviolable rights of the individual and the preservation of human dignity. It had sacrificed the idea of humanity as weak and incompatible with its heroic attitude, it had paralysed the feeling for freedom because it held that subordination to a whole was more fundamental and important.

The right-wing anti-democratic movement was bourgeois, but it despised the middle class and its nineteenth-century political

achievements. The German middle-class citizen's one-time re-
moteness from politics—for which Thomas Mann had put up
such a splendid defence in his *Betrachtungen eines Unpolitischen*
—became a hysterical plunge into the political sphere where
ignorance was matched by a sense of romantic adventure.
Though rich in ideas and full of intellectual energy, the Conservative Revolution finally became little more than the stooge
of National Socialism because in its preoccupation with wild
polemic and its own fanciful ideas it had failed to take to
heart the realities of political life and of human beings in society.
Ernst Jünger once wrote that it was highly enjoyable to take
part in intellectual high-treason against the intellect. The result
of this attitude was finally a high degree of intellectual impotence
in coping with the power of unreason which triumphed in
National Socialism.

It is certainly true that the Republic was unattractive and
unglamorous, weak and disunited, that it lacked almost everything which could arouse the support and enthusiasm of young
people. But surely its miserable state was a reason to reconcile
ideas with reality, to come to its intellectual support instead of
condemning it continually and thereby making it weaker?

There were few, or at any rate too few intellectuals in the
Germany of that time who were prepared to adopt this attitude.
The intellectual Left was republican in outlook, but hardly less
critical of the Weimar state than the Right. The Right believed
it held the master-ideas of the twentieth century and dreamt of a
special mission for Germany in the world. Its decisive weakness
which no amount of good will could cancel was its irrationalism.
Nothing is more dangerous in political life than the surrender of
reason. The intellect must remain the controlling and regulating
authority in life. The anti-democratic intellectuals of the Weimar
period betrayed the intellect to life—they despised reason and
found more truth in myth or in the coursing of their blood-
stream. In every case anti-democratic reality has less suggestive
and intoxicating power than many anti-democratic ideas. Given
more reason and enlightenment, those intellectuals would perhaps have seen more clearly where their zeal was leading them
and the German people.

In retrospect, for all its power and intensity this world of
ideas appears sterile and abortive—though it had fateful political
consequences. After 1945 we had to return to the liberal demo-

cratic constitution and Thomas Mann was completely right when he wrote before the Nazis seized power: "The anti-democratic nationalist movement judges this century quite wrongly in believing that it is determined only by its own tendencies, for it overlooks the fact that the aspirations which it now despises and condemns are at least as important for the life of this century as itself and that without the spiritual and ethical content which the word freedom embraces men are not men and cannot live as human beings."

ERICH MATTHIAS

Social Democracy and the Power in the State

Professor Erich Matthias was born in 1921. He studied history at Göttingen and Munich from 1939 to 1940, resuming his studies in 1945 and taking his degree in 1951. He is Professor of Political Science at Marburg and head of the research unit in Bonn of the Commission for the History of Parliamentarianism and Political Parties. His publications include a number of historical and political works.

Natural as it is for us to speak of 30th January, 1933, as the day when the Nazis seized power, it would not occur to us to talk of a Social Democratic seizure of power in November, 1918. Yet the real power which then fell to the Social Democrats was much greater than the measure of control over the apparatus of state which originally accompanied Hitler's appointment as Reich Chancellor. But whereas the Nazis, as soon as the door opened a crack, seized one position of power after another with breath-taking speed and from the first moment left no doubt at all that they considered the whole state as their well-deserved booty, the Social Democrat deputies of 1918 only used the dictatorial powers which accrued to them as a temporary bridge to cover the three-month period between the outbreak of the revolution and the meeting of the national constituent assembly.

But though this behaviour contrasts favourably with the unscrupulous misuse of power by the National Socialist victors of 1933, it would be a mistake to present the moderation of the Social Democrats as a model of democratic self-control.

It is often maintained that the Weimar Republic was necessarily condemned to failure because of the opportunities missed during those three months. Though this thesis is not tenable the question nevertheless remains whether it was not within the power of the Social Democrat leaders of that time to create a more stable democratic foundation for the young republic.

That the task which thrust itself upon them was difficult, perhaps even insoluble, requires no discussion. Nevertheless, it can be shown that many a measure which might have served to anchor the new democracy more firmly was omitted, not so much because it was impracticable, but because even in the changed conditions many of the leading men still derived the criteria for their actions from the limited field of pre-war Social Democracy's views and experiences. This fact supplies the key to an historical judgement on the passivity of Social Democratic policy during the November revolution and in the early days of the Weimar Republic. From here, too, opens a way to understanding the political helplessness of the SPD during the break-up of the republic. For the traditionalistic paralysis which, despite many fruitful attempts, the party was unable to throw off to the bitter end limited its choice of action much more than the unfavourable circumstances to which Social Democratic spokesmen kept referring. In this respect the words of Party Chairman Otto Wels were characteristic when at the Paris Congress of the Socialist Workers' International in August, 1933, he tried to excuse the destruction of the Social Democrats at the hands of the Nazis by saying: "We were driven by the force of circumstances to a much greater degree than the parties of any other country. We were really only the victims of developments."

But the historical observer can hardly agree to exculpate the Social Democratic Party with its millions of supporters on the grounds that it was the innocent, defenceless victim of all-powerful circumstances. He will rather be forced to the conclusion that Otto Wels' statement faithfully mirrors the spirit of resignation which possessed the Social Democrats and that it was this spirit which made them mere "victims of developments" and led them to their own downfall and the downfall of the republic.

From this it is already clear that responsibility for the failure of the Weimar Republic and the parties which supported it cannot be placed exclusively on Adolf Hitler and the notorious enemies of the republic. It is equally wrong to transfer the main weight of responsibility to exterior factors. Neither the attitude of the powers which had emerged victorious from the First World War, nor the effects of the Treaty of Versailles nor the sudden impact of the world economic crisis were prime causes of the disintegration of the democratic system. The comfortable excuse that in view of the situation nothing could stand up to the dynamic mass movement of National Socialism will not bear serious examination. We need only recall that Hitler became Reich Chancellor at a time when the economic crisis was beginning to abate and politically the radicalised masses were becoming disabused. The events of those times threw into relief the decisive part played by the overtaxed and senile Reich President and the harmful influence of his formally irresponsible advisers and this very fact draws one's attention to the failure of the party system and its progressive impotence.

None of the groups involved can be acquitted of some share in the responsibility. The heavy guilt incurred by the Com-

munists and the German Nationalists whose suicidal course
helped no one but the Nazis does not clear the other central
parties of blame. All the non-Nazi and anti-Nazi forces had only
one feature in common, an inability to form a realistic picture of
the danger which threatened them and the methods of their
totalitarian opponent. This was largely responsible for their re-
luctance to compromise and for a confusion of fronts in which
the contrasts "bourgeois-Socialist", "democratic-totalitarian"
and "republican-antirepublican" became entangled and super-
imposed. As the popular conservative experiment proved a
failure and the liberal parties were squeezed out and sank to
insignificance, only the Social Democrats and the Centre remained as the potential core of democratic defence against
totalitarianism. But even the big Catholic party which had
undergone a swing to the right under the leadership of Kaas and
Brüning did not prove immune to the advancing authoritarian
tendencies.

On the other hand, Social Democracy can claim to have remained to the bitter end the strongest and most consistent force
of parliamentary democracy in Germany and to have been the
only party in the republic to have maintained uncompromising
opposition to rising National Socialism. This should be stressed
particularly as the present-day SPD is involved much more
directly in the question of responsibility for the failure of the
Weimar Republic than the other more recently founded parties
which possess no unbroken historical tradition and therefore cannot be directly identified with their predecessors.

For this very reason Social Democracy should not evade an
examination of its own past. When it is reproached in the political battles of the present for its record in the concluding phase
of the Weimar period it possesses excellent arguments to rebut
such attacks. But nothing would be more dangerous than to
confuse a justifiable reference to the democratic integrity shown
by the old party with an acquittal from any historical responsibility. If historical experiences are to prove of value to the
cause of democracy nothing deserves greater attention than the
democrats' own share of responsibility.

A clear failure on the part of Social Democracy was already
evident at the start of the final phase and in the spring of 1930
this occasioned the break-up of the Grand Coalition. However,
the measure of responsibility emerging from this state of affairs

should not be rated too highly, for here in particular *occasion* and *cause* should not be confused. The main cause of the government's collapse was the class war which had direct effects at government and parliamentary level and drove the parties at both extremes of the coalition asunder. But the war was fought much more stubbornly by the right-wing liberal *Deutsche Volkspartei* than by the Social Democrats. So the only reproach which can be levelled at the SPD at this stage is that, committed to a trade union policy supported by the party's left wing, it showed a lack of tactical skill in unnecessarily incurring the odium of splitting the government over a battle for a $\frac{1}{2}$ per cent increase in the contribution for unemployment insurance. This reproach weighs lightly when one recalls, for instance, the consequences of Brüning's frivolous dissolution of the Reichstag in July, 1930, after the SPD had offered its co-operation and he had curtly rejected it. Moreover, the tactical failure in the spring of 1930 was more than made good by the sense of responsibility and readiness for sacrifice shown by the SPD in the period of toleration.

But the break-up of the Grand Coalition was a decisive turning-point in that it represented an act of self-exclusion by the parties which brought the chronic structural crisis of the party state into the open and initiated the visible dissolution of the democratic system. But at no time did this process acquire the character of inevitablity. It only became irreversible when the parties accepted the loss of power they had suffered and gave up any serious attempt to revive the paralysed mechanism of parliamentary democracy. The abandonment of Hermann Müller's practically isolated government by the Social Democrats was not necessarily in itself even a political mistake. Their real failure rather lay in the fact that they had no political plan for themselves either in power or in opposition. Their withdrawal from the coalition was not the prelude to a new policy but an escape into noisy opposition without tangible aims, an opposition after the pre-war pattern notable for a hopeless lack of constructive initiative and tactical elasticity.

This attitude was determined by that lack of a realistic relationship to power which still clung to the Social Democrats as their most fateful heritage from the period of their development in Imperial Germany. It had been and still was the dilemma of the SPD that they had no conception of the possibilities open to them for exerting their influence and had never learnt to realise their potential power politically. This becomes particularly clear when we turn to the period in which Brüning's government was tolerated: it was obvious then that the Social Democrats still represented a considerable weight in the scales of democracy, but equally obviously their weight was a passive one.

At the Reichstag elections of 14th September, 1930, the National Socialists suddenly became the second largest party in the Reichstag and the Communists also scored remarkable gains. According to the prevailing view this made the formation of a working parliamentary majority impossible. On the other hand, recently discovered sources suggest that the "grand coalition of all reasonable elements" called for immediately after the elections by the Social Democrat Prime Minister of Prussia Otto Braun might well have been brought about. Although Brüning had conducted the electoral campaign in stark opposition to the Social Democrats his first reaction to the alarming results was, as we now know, not very different from the Prussian Prime Minister's. It may seem even more surprising that leading industrial circles, to which the scope of the National Socialist success had come as a serious shock, now suddenly began to demand a coalition with the Social Democrats. Geheimrat Kastl, for instance, of the Association of Germany Industry expressed his "concern about further political developments" only a day after the elections and wished to bring to the notice of the Reich Chancellor that the Association was "absolutely" of the opinion that the government must obtain wide parliamentary support for its programme of reforms in the new Reichstag, "which in the present situation can only be with the co-operation of the Left". A good week later, Franz von Papen wrote to his friend Schleicher about a long conversation he had had with the Chancellor: "The bankers are clamouring at Brüning's door— and mostly those who gave election money to the Nazis are wailing now for the immediate formation of the Grand Coalition."

The question why, in these circumstances, not even an attempt was made to form a majority government extending further to the left cannot be discussed here in all its varied aspects. As regards Brüning's attitude it may be noted that he gave fateful precedence in his mind to the deflationary cure which he intended to continue unchanged and regardless of internal dangers. What he wanted from the parties was not so much co-operation as non-interference in the continuation of the policy which he himself repeatedly called "practical". Even the extension of the government to the left which at first had been planned was only intended to serve as a parliamentary flank-guard for this bureaucratic and technically refined policy. But when secret discussions with the leaders of the Social Democratic Party revealed that the same effect could be achieved without Social Democrats entering the government Brüning believed he had every cause for satisfaction because in this way he avoided the embarrassment of having to choose between the SPD and the moderate right-wing forces who opposed the inclusion of Social Democrats in the government.

But far from associating themselves with the Prussian Prime Minister Braun's demand, the leaders of the SPD had made no attempt after the elections to use their 143 votes to claim an active share in the government. Nothing casts more light on the situation than that Brüning and the Social Democratic leaders met half way in their efforts to avoid a real political decision. This means in effect that the stock motivation put forward by the Social Democrats for their behaviour, namely that toleration of Brüning's government was the "lesser evil" compared with overt dictatorship or a strongly right-wing government, though not wrong is incomplete as an explanation. One would have to add that the party preferred this solution, which meant neither coalition nor opposition, not only to the consequences of a frivolous defeat of the Brüning government, but also to a firm connection with that government in the form of a coalition which would have kept it in office.

Their toleration of the Brüning cabinet robbed the Social Democrats of all tactical scope. They found themselves obliged to accept the most unpopular cuts and emergency measures though these were passionately rejected by their supporters and they even had to let laws pass which bestowed one-sided benefits on agriculture. Even when the "National Opposition" withdrew from the Reichstag in February, 1931, not returning until the autumn session, the Social Democrats did not exploit their temporarily strengthened position.

In the period between the September elections of 1930 and the fall of Brüning the Social Democrats showed how far they had allowed the initiative to slip from their hands. Apart from the Catholic parties and the small *Staatspartei* they proved throughout this whole period to be the most reliable parliamentary supporters of the cabinet, but without being able to obtain more than small concessions in return, largely in the sphere of social politics. When an oppositional Social Democrat newspaper stated maliciously in the spring of 1931 that Brüning knew "how to tame the grumbling Social Democrats" and only needed to threaten with his or Hindenburg's resignation to make the leaders of the Reichstag fraction "as mild as a dove" the words were felt to be offensive just because they came so near to the truth. Records of the rare conversations between representatives of the SPD fraction and the Reich Chancellor show the Social Democrats, who revealed an astonishing degree of modesty on such occasions, less in the role of partners in political negotiations than of suppliants at some government office.

Although this state of affairs must have been found depressing no action was taken to bring the parliamentary potential of the Social Democrats more effectively to bear, and though they held a heavy share of responsibility for the measures of the Brüning government increasing unemployment and deterioration of the economic situation still found them drawing modest consolation from the fact that no Social Democrat minister was in the cabinet—and this because they felt better able to withstand the competition of the Communists and the pressure from their own left wing through the half measure of toleration than if they had become a direct government party.

All efforts to develop a powerful programme to fight the economic crisis and unemployment came to naught because the leaders and economists among the Social Democrats were excessively afraid of inflation. After conscientiously examining the situation they came to the conclusion that there was no "general recipe" for overcoming the crisis. As in 1918, all "experiments" and any departure from the path of democratic legality were rejected on principle. So the Social Democrats could put forward no alternative of their own to the deflationary policy of the government. They could see no other course but to defend the workers' standard of living as best they could and hope that the economic crisis would abate. Paradoxically the Social Democrats pinned their hopes on a recovery of the capitalist economy. Once the economy was functioning normally again the constitutional framework of the republic would recover its solidity. This, roughly, was the thought behind the Social Democrats' policy

5—TRTD

of tolerating the Brüning government; it was a policy in which a sense of responsibility and readiness for self-sacrifice was combined with deep perplexity and a passive self-exclusion from affairs.

Behind the negative aims of this policy which sought to tie down the Centre and the bourgeois parties and keep the National Socialists away from power there lay, however, an unbroken determination to defend Social Democracy itself and this was backed by the strong party organisation and the positions of power which still remained to it, particularly in Prussia.

Despite the party's small ability to attract fresh support and the pressures it had to endure, surprisingly enough its internal structure remained strong. To the very end the National Socialists barely broke into its pool of supporters and up to March, 1933, a hard core of over seven million voters stayed loyal to the SPD.

Admittedly, the split in the party which first began to show at the Leipzig Party Day in May, 1931, could not be entirely prevented. But the Socialist Workers' Party which had been newly founded in October, 1931, was not able to play a part in politics, nor did it succeed in shaking the stability of the Social Democratic Party organisation which still included nearly a million members in the second half of 1932. Despite the founding of the Socialist Workers' Party and the much more dangerous attraction of the Communist Party for the despairing unemployed the number of organised Social Democrats had only dropped by about 65,000 since 1st January, 1931, and it was still about 35,000 higher than at the end of 1928.

In no other political group did an appeal to party discipline have such a lasting effect as in Social Democracy. The average Social Democrat was prepared to accept great demands on his loyalty without leaving the organisation. Unity and cohesion in the party was not only looked on as a practical necessity for political success, but represented first and foremost something of emotional value, a sublime feeling divorced from practical affairs which gave life in the Social Democratic organisations its leaven and largely determined its character. But even this only partially explains the solidity of the party structure, still less the fidelity of the electors.

It was of decisive importance for the maintenance of internal cohesion in the SPD that the depressing impotence of Social

Democracy after 14th September, 1930, was overlaid by a wave
of belligerent impulses which deeply stirred the party's daily life.
The immediate reaction of the Social Democratic masses to the
Nazi electoral victory brought about not a weakening, but a
strengthening of the will to defend the republic. "For the first
time", writes Julius Leber, "the Social Democratic rank and file
felt strong dissatisfaction with their own leaders." The feeling
gained ground that traditional parliamentary methods were inadequate and while the party continued to turn "in the circle
of its own irresolution" the young activists thronged into the
streets to show the Nazi civil-warmongers that they were ready
to fight in defence of the republic.

The backbone of the will to resist was supplied by the officially
non-party democratic *Reichsbanner* organisation which had been
founded by the SPD, the Centre and the Democrats as a republican ex-soldiers' association and in effect became a Social
Democratic force for the defence of the republic. As early as
20th September, 1930, the leaders of the *Reichsbanner* decided
to organise a picked body of fighting troops and barely six
months later, after making their public appearance in mass rallies
throughout Germany, the defence formations, or *Schufo** as they
were called, numbered 160,000 men. By the following spring
they must have totalled at least 250,000. The *Schufo* represented
the militant core, but at the end of 1931 an "Iron Front" was
set up by the SPD, the free trade unions and the workers' sport
organisations as a direct response to the "Harzburg Front" of
the anti-republican right-wingers and this revealed the extent of
the will to defend the republic.

There is no doubt that this organisation canalised fresh impulses that were thrusting up from below. But though the mass
rallies of the "Iron Front" supplied an impressive picture of the
Social Democratic workers' readiness for action it is difficult to
draw general conclusions about the state of training of the
Reichsbanner formations or the extent of the preparations made
for the forceful prevention of a National Socialist *coup d'état*.
What certainly did not exist was an adequate co-ordination of
the measures planned and prepared in different places and by
different authorities. And certainly a good deal of romanticism
and self-deception was involved in all this. But that does not alter
the fact that there was a genuine readiness at that time amongst

* *Schutzformationen.*

many members of the organisations included in the "Iron Front"
to stake their lives if need be in the defence of the republic.

When after Brüning's fall the new Chancellor von Papen prepared to strike at Prussia the time for action seemed to have
arrived. But the leaders of the Social Democrats and the Iron
Front decided not to oppose this clear and open breach of the
constitution—a decision that had fateful consequences even after
the republican "fortress" of Prussia proved untenable, for, as
Julius Leber wrote a year later in prison, that 20th July, 1932,
"which revealed the whole inner weakness and indecision of the
Weimar Front", directly prepared the way for 30th January,
1933, and the seizure of total power by the National Socialists.

Nothing sheds more light on this course of events than the diary
of Joseph Goebbels, chief propagandist of the Nazi Party and
Gauleiter of Berlin. On 21st July he was already noting : "The
Reds have missed their big chance. It will never recur."

The action against the government of Prussia did not come
unexpectedly. Since the beginning of June, the National Socialists and the German Nationalists had been pressing for the
appointment of a Reich Commissioner and the new Reich
government under Papen was seen to be looking for pretexts to
justify the step.

If ever there was a moment when the "Iron Front" should
have taken action it was on the day when the National Socialists or the "reactionary" Papen cabinet which was felt to be
submissive to them proceeded to carry out the coup against
Prussia. As things lay, the masses ready to defend the republic
made no distinction between Hitler's lust for power and the
thinly camouflaged plans of Papen and Schleicher who had
allowed the SA onto the streets again.

The optimism and reviving self-confidence of their supporters
in whom the impressive mass demonstrations and rallies of the
"Iron Front" had aroused a deceptive feeling of strength at least
infected the party leaders to the extent that they toyed with
the idea of resistance; but at the decisive moment the respon-
sible-minded Social Democrat politicians who took pride in their
"realism" felt that the objections were too weighty. Reared in a
party hierarchy which for decades had avoided risks involving
the smallest incalculable consequence filled with panicky
distaste for all "experiments" and reluctant from a long humanitarian tradition to shed blood, they consoled themselves and their

supporters with the approaching Reichstag elections. The possibility in this situation of appealing in the age-old manner to the power of the ballot paper seemed to them to be the most proper and desirable course. So they appealed to their supporters to do nothing which might interfere with the holding of elections on 31st July.

As the attempts to pacify them made by their leaders and the party press indirectly confirm, an immense agitation prevailed among the members of the "Iron Front". That they took no spontaneous action was probably due to the discipline of the Social Democrat supporters.

It is impossible to assess accurately the state of readiness of the *Reichsbanner* and the workers' organisations on 20th July. But despite the lack or inadequacy of weapons and despite considerable regional and local differences the militant élite formations of the *Reichsbanner* can be looked on as the core of the will to resist. They certainly wished to be more actively employed than as bodyguards at political meetings and in the critical hours they were waiting at their assembly points for a call from their leaders.

If there had been a civil war, the possibility that the "Iron Front" would have closed firmly round its militant core at least cannot be excluded *a priori*. But two conditions would have had to have been fulfilled: a rapid decision exploiting the spontaneous indignation by the party and trade union leaders and the co-operation of the Prussian police whose loyalty was never put to the test. For this, the attitude of the leading police officials was less important than that of the Prussian Prime Minister Braun and his Minister of the Interior Severing, both of whom were accounted strong men. The excuses since made on their behalf—that a battle to "restore a competent ministry" and revolt against a "decree issued by the Reich President" were not inspiring goals—would have been incomprehensible in the state of excitement then prevailing. The older men, too, looked to them as their appointed leaders in the battle to defend the republic. Their vote would also have had some influence on the sober and disciplined Social Democrat industrial workers whose readiness for battle had been considerably underestimated by party and trade union leaders when they decided against a general strike. A temporary close-down of vital factories and an interruption of rail transport, such as was planned by the union of railway workers, would probably have been well within the bounds of possibility.

All in all, an impressive revolt could have taken place and this would have put the Reich President and the leaders of the *Reichswehr*, both of whom detested the thought of civil war, in a difficult position. To decree a precautionary state of emergency was not the same thing as accepting full responsibility for mass slaughter. The thought suggests itself that in supporting the *coup d'état* in Prussia General von Schleicher was working on the assumption that the Left would probably not be prepared to shoulder the full risk of a civil war so that it would suffice to use the *Reichswehr* to influence and threaten without forcing it to surrender its "non-party attitude" which was largely fictional anyway. If this was General Schleicher's view an unexpectedly determined demonstration of readiness for civil war on the part of the Left could have become a decisive factor in the political situation despite the clear military superiority of the *Reichswehr*. For as things lay, political imponderables were no less important than force of arms. It was only the resigned attitude of the Social Democrats and the clear proof of their deficient will to power on 20th July, 1932, which wrote off the party as a serious political factor. Moreover, it is characteristic of the mentality of the Social Democrat leaders that a secret fear of the consequences of victory, however improbable, no doubt set the seal on their inability to reach a decision. A battle for political power outside the usual parliamentary channels had no legitimate place in their world of ideas although its political outcome for the defenders of democracy would by no means have been exhausted with the alternatives of victory or defeat.

However uncertain the ground which this survey covers, one thing is definite: with 20th July the last chance was thrown away of extending the basis of republican resistance to the right and left, and the results of total failure could not have been more disastrous than the political and psychological consequences of inactivity.

The 20th July hit the "Iron Front" at its most sensitive spot: it shook the naïvely trusting confidence of its supporters and thereby robbed it of its inner strength. Under the influence of discipline and tradition the electoral strength of the party was maintained fairly well over the July elections and up till March, 1933, but in the background a creeping paralysis was spreading through the party and becoming a mirror of its leaders' own passivity.

More than ever before the SPD was now isolated. The rallies staged by the "Iron Front" mainly served as a sedative; recruits could no longer be attracted by a purely defensive policy. The fact, however, that the much vaunted "organisation" still held together as though nothing had happened prevented a mood of panic arising among the leaders or their followers. Many of those responsible did not properly understand the magnitude of their decision on 20th July. Even after that date, Leipart, the trade union chairman, and Hans Vogel, the second chairman of the party, are said to have declared that they need only press the button to start the mechanism of resistance.

So the last defenders of the written constitution and of the parliamentary system that had long since failed held out apparently unmoved on their Social Democratic island of tradition. As they resignedly watched the stream of events flowing round and past them they drew comfort from the knowledge of their own solidarity.

It was thanks to the automatic loyalty of its supporters that a source of resistance was still present in the "Iron Front" despite the more or less open crisis of confidence provoked by 20th July. The key formations of the *Reichsbanner* in particular maintained to the very end a stubborn determination to offer resistance, though the feeling had penetrated their ranks, too, that they were defending a hopeless cause.

When on 30th January, 1933, indignation fired those still possessed of the will to resist, the same gulf was revealed as on 20th July in the previous year between the spontaneous urge for deeds among the activists of the "Iron Front" and the indecision and inertia of their leaders. Though opposition by the Social Democrats alone seemed to offer no prospect of success after 30th January, the following months up to the official ban on the party showed once again and with particular clarity the symptoms which had brought about the tragic failure of Social Democracy in the years of the great crisis. All the same, it must be noted that none of the anti-Nazi forces operating at that time showed more courage and foresight than the last isolated defenders of the Weimar system who opposed the National Socialist Enabling Bill. Nevertheless, Social Democratic policy as a whole in this period gives the impression of passive drift, the main object being apparently to preserve the party organisation in its existing form and help it to survive crisis or catastrophe. This raises a question which is still of importance for the SPD revived after 1945 and should be more vital for self-understanding than the effort to dissociate itself from an ideological "Marxism" which even for the old party was not much more than a placard. We mean the question of the traditional modes of behaviour of Social Democracy in which certain definite traits can be detected, determined primarily by the rigidity of Social Democratic thought. The characteristics of this thought which was revealed particularly clearly in the catastrophe of the workers' movement can be described as follows:

1. The institutionalised thought tied to the traditional party apparatus and the forms of struggle it had practised for decades led to the Social Democratic organisations of the workers' movement being looked on not as a means to an end, but as an end in themselves. This thoroughly conservative attitude to organisation induced the Social Democrats to overestimate their own strength, encouraged complacency and self-sufficiency, blinded them to the real dangers and paralysed political initiative because it preferred the maintenance of the organisation to the taking of political risks.

2. To institutionalised thought in the categories of the parliamentary party state and a constitutional system no other than a parliamentary system was conceivable, unless it was a return to the pre-war authoritarian state.

3. Social Democracy, which had grown up as a legal parliamentary party but officially still clung to its revolutionary and Socialist character, needed to maintain extremely strong internal discipline. Only in this way was it possible to demonstrate effectively the power of the masses and at the same time preclude any unwelcome spontaneous interference with parliamentary action. It was in keeping with the spirit of the party that it was led by officials. The dilemma of 20th July, 1932, and of 30th January, 1933, consisted in the fact that the leaders' intellectual cast made them incapable of taking the initiative while on the other hand the resolute activists in the "Iron Front" looked trustingly to their leaders because party discipline forbade them to act on their own.

4. The evolutionist thought sprang principally from the experience of the party's steady growth in Imperial Germany and

the myth arising from it that it was indestructible despite all temporary reverses. This line of thought, misleadingly called "Marxist" and "revolutionary", fulfilled its traditional function even in the midst of catastrophe; it justified passivity and gave new confidence because it promised that the victorious reactionary and totalitarian opponents would destroy themselves.

5. Humanitarian thought, which had become widespread through the workers' education movement, corresponded to the pacifist views prevailing in the party and fostered an unrealistic faith in reason. The people imbued with this thought confronted the dynamic mass movement of National Socialism without understanding for the irrational elements which go to form a political purpose and in the midst of catastrophe they still relied on "intellectual superiority" as a means of conducting the fight.

The tenacity of the thought-structure typified by these norms sprang largely from the fact that since the lapse of the anti-Socialist law of 1890 party work continued without interruption or challenge in the same channels. The shock of 1933 was needed before the painful process of reassessment could begin and the struggle for a new political realism has undoubtedly continued since 1945 in the newly founded party. But the fact should not be overlooked that for many faithful Social Democrats the new party represented from the start a revival of the old one to which they returned after mental exile. Therewith from the very first hour of the new party's life the spirit of tradition and restoration reasserted itself and for this spirit the events of 1933 still represented an unavoidable natural catastrophe.

RUDOLF MORSEY

The Centre Party between the Fronts

Rudolf Morsey was born in 1927. He took history and German studies at Münster where he obtained a Doctorate of Philosophy in 1955. After two years of schoolmastering he became a scientific collaborator of the Commission for the History of Parliamentarianism and Political Parties in Bonn. He has written a number of books on German political history and has made a special study of the relationship between Church and State since the Bismarck period.

The Weimar Republic was certainly not lacking in events which even contemporaries recognised as historically significant. Among the turning points in the fourteen-year history of the Republic belongs 27th March, 1930, when the "Grand Coalition" stretching from the Social Democrats to the *Deutsche Volkspartei* under Reich Chancellor Hermann Müller broke apart and Reich President von Hindenburg called on the Centre politician Heinrich Brüning, then aged forty-four, to become the new Reich Chancellor. Brüning accepted the post and also the condition attached to it that he should form a right-wing government independent of the parliamentary majority. On 30th March, 1930, began the era of "Presidential governments" based on the confidence of the Reich President and his extraordinary constitutional rights. Because of the relative strengths of the parties there was to be no going back from them to a parliamentary democracy functioning in the spirit of the Weimar constitution. As an acknowledged financial expert and chairman of the Centre fraction in the Reichstag Brüning was one of the leading parliamentarians, but hitherto he had not held public office or attracted much attention to himself and his nomination seemed to inaugurate a new epoch in the history of the German Centre party.

Since 1870 this party had primarily represented the interests of the German Catholics and after the revolution of 1918 it had not found it at all easy to adapt itself to the republic. Owing to the split-off of the Bavarian People's Party (1919-20) and the movement of Catholic voters into other political camps the Centre was not able to maintain its previous body of supporters. It could not capture more than 13 per cent of the total electorate (of which 60 per cent were women) or, together with the Bavarian People's Party, more than 17 per cent in 1924 or 15 per cent in 1932. Nevertheless, since 1919, as a stabilising element in the different Weimar coalitions this "born middle party" had given positive proof of its ability to govern. In the words of the party historian Carl Bechem the Centre embraced all classes and was therefore in a position to "reconcile the inevitable conflicts of interest even within its own ranks".

But the central position in the framework of the Weimar constellation of parties and the formation of coalitions extending to the Left and Right in no way represented the unanimous desire of the party leaders or of the electorate that supported it. There was unity concerning the rejection of Marxist Socialism—which was logical from the religious standpoint—but disunity about the degree of democratisation worth striving for, about giving whole-hearted support to the Weimar Republic—which no party particularly loved—and on the question, how far it was admissible to surrender basic points in the party programme for the sake of maintaining the coalition. Owing to the domination of Wilhelm Marx, party chairman since 1921 and for many years Reich Chancellor, by his "conservative" associates, a coalition came about in January, 1927, with the German Nationalist People's Party which was hostile to the republic. The attempt to reconcile the "nationalist right wing" with the republic by bringing it into the government was combined with the hope of setting the seal on the inclusion of Catholicism in the German national consciousness. It was expected that this government would solve certain cultural questions of importance to the Centre, amongst them the provision of a Reich school law.

But the alliance with the German Nationalists only raised difficulties for the Centre Party. It led to severe internal dissension because the permanent coalition with the SPD in Prussia was continued. Aided by other factors this dual policy led to a serious crisis which weakened solidarity. As a result the Centre lost seven mandates at the Reichstag elections of 20th May, 1928. Abandonment of the right-wing coalition and membership of the "Grand Coalition" cabinet under the Social Democrat Reich Chancellor Hermann Müller created fresh dissensions and allegiances. Against the background of these internal tensions the election of a new party chairman took place at a party conference in December, 1928, in Cologne. In the prevailing conflict of interests only the election of a prelate, the well-known expert on ecclesiastical law Ludwig Kaas, seemed able to bring about the necessary compromise. Under his leadership the last phase in the sixty-year history of the Centre Party began.

Within the party a process of soul-searching started at once combined with an intensification of the religious element. The party strove to achieve a stronger ideological uniformity and self-assurance. From 1929 a new course became apparent deter-

mined by the "conservative" wing of the party which became
dominant under Kaas and Brüning, the latter taking over leadership of the fraction. In the deepening crisis of German parliamentarianism and the multi-party state this course aimed at
strengthening the structure of the state and the authority of the
government under the concept of the *Volksgemeinschaft*, or
community of the people, which soon afterwards was distorted
to suit the National Socialists. In the Centre Party the call arose
for a political leader who should be independent of the Reichstag which had become incapable of action owing to the disrup-
tion of the parties.

The coalition government under the weak Reich Chancellor
Hermann Müller was felt to be a "cabinet of indecision and
weakness". In a speech in Dortmund on 17th October, 1929,
Kaas called for a government which should be "more independent of the incalculable variations of the political barometer". A
few weeks later, the leading Centrist politician Eugen Bolz
criticised the "impotence of our whole system of government"
which was no longer able to solve the most urgent political
problems. Such statements characterised a general unease at the
failure of the multi-party state and "formal democracy" and
the search for new paths outside the ineffective parliamentary
method of government. In this respect the intentions of the
Centrist leaders coincided with those of Hindenburg and his
advisers.

The Reich President wanted to have the course "swing to the
right". He believed he could entrust Brüning with the leadership of a new-style "Presidential cabinet". The Centre greeted
the appointment of the prominent deputy to the Reich Chancellorship with joy, believing it to be the beginning of a new era
which would see the "restoration of a healthy parliamentarianism". At this time it could not be foreseen that in supporting the new government the party would incur the odium for
Brüning's unpopular and ineffective emergency policies. The
Centre moved further and further away from its previous coalition partners, but without being able to gain new allies among
the numerically weak moderate right-wing groups or to form
stable majorities. The party gradually fell between two fronts
and between these in different circumstances it was finally
crushed in the summer of 1933.

There was an inner connection between the effects of the world economic crisis in Germany and the deepening crisis of parliamentarianism. Brüning's one-sided policy of deflation and governing by emergency decree and his mistake in dissolving the two-year-old Reichstag on 18th July, 1930, led to the so-called "catastrophic elections" of 14th September, 1930, which amounted to a parliamentary landslide. A leap in the representation of the Nazi Party which instead of twelve now sent 107 deputies to the Reichstag, marked success by the Communists and further losses by the democratic middle parties—of which only the Centre remained unaffected—bore witness to the dwindling power of parliamentary democracy. As the formation of a constructive majority seemed impossible as a consequence and as Brüning declined to enter a coalition with the Social Democrats—which was a feasible proposition—it only remained to continue with the previous government which was independent of parliament and only reluctantly tolerated by the SPD. Though the Centre Party supported this course as a matter of principle it was clear to everyone that it could only provide a temporary solution. A political joke was current at that time: "Why is Brüning like a guitar?" Answer: "Because he is held by the left hand and strummed by the right."

Since the turn of the year 1930-31, the chairman of the Centre Party, Prelate Kaas, had been propounding the idea of a "popular assembly" in which those political groups should come together "for a limited time and specific purposes" which had previously not co-operated. This idea of an assembly which Kaas extended during the crisis of 1932 into a passionate demand for a non-party "emergency fellowship" aimed at an *ad hoc* political alliance for a specified period with the inclusion of the National Socialists. They were to be "tamed" and "canalised" by sharing in political and parliamentary responsibility. The faulty estimate inherent in this idea of Hitler and his totalitarian aspirations as well as of the aims and dynamism of the anti-democratic Nazi mass movement was shared by the Centre with almost all the middle-class party leaders and also with the Reich President.

Hindenburg's re-election in the spring of 1932 was primarily due to Brüning. The Reich Chancellor had not accepted suggestions that he should stand himself for the office of Reich President and taking the realistic view that apart from Hinden-

burg no other candidate of the middle parties would stand a
chance against Adolf Hitler backed by the Nazi Party and, in
the second ballot, by the German Nationalists, the Centre Party
supported the re-election of the aged Field-Marshal. In doing
so, it embarked on the prevailing wave of emotion, called
Hindenburg a "proven and heroic figure" and even went so far
as to proclaim him "the God-sent saviour of the German
nation". The reward for Brüning's strong personal efforts to
secure Hindenburg's re-election (on 10th April, 1932) came only
a few weeks later. On 30th May, the Reich President, influenced
by his irresponsible advisers, dismissed the Chancellor in so
brusque a manner that Brüning never got over the affront to his
feelings or the lack of political motivation. And when, of all
people, Franz von Papen accepted the Chancellorship indignation in the Centre Party knew no bounds.

After twelve years' participation in the government and the
responsibilities of government it came as a terrible shock to be
thrust overnight into the unaccustomed status of an opposition
party. Moreover, the Centre was confronted with a Chancellor
who for years as a deputy in the Prussian *Landtag* had been
accounted a member of their party. But the party was given no
time to watch the first steps of the new government which aimed
at abolishing the parliamentarianism of Weimar. On 4th June,
Papen persuaded the Reich President to dissolve the Reichstag
"in order to clarify internal affairs", as the government statement
declared.

Any other Chancellor would have had a less provocative effect
on the Centre than Papen who had acquired the reputation of
a renegade and whose nomination Brüning had been unable to
prevent. The party's disapproval of the "cabinet of the barons"
was apparent at once. On 31st May, the Centrist leaders Kaas
and Perlitius warned the Reich President against a "partial solution". They demanded a "total solution", in other words a clear
acceptance of responsibility by the right-wing parties with the
inclusion of the Nazi Party in the government. The deputy chairman of the Centre, Joseph Joos, declared on 8th June: "Seldom
has the fall of a government created such a stir in the country
as that of Brüning's cabinet. . . . Those who don't know at least
suspect that forces have emerged here out of the darkness of
political irresponsibility and that they may lead us into darkness."

6—TRTD

In contrast to the intentions of this "short-term" government the Centrist leaders proclaimed their aim to be the creation of a strong block "broadly based on the forces supporting the people's state and the people's community". The Secretary General of the Centre, Heinrich Vockel, called for an electoral campaign for a bigger and stronger German Centre Party.

But this goal which was to be achieved through the elections to the new Reichstag seemed more distant than ever when, on 31st July, 1932, the Nazis increased their mandates from 107 to 230 and, in an unholy alliance with the Communists, were now able to apply in the Reichstag the parliamentary obstruction they had practised in the Prussian House of Deputies.

Through the disappearance of the bourgeois middle parties the Centre with its seventy-five deputies once again occupied a key position between the nationalist and the Marxist forces. A coalition with the Nazi Party could have replaced the Papen government by one based on a parliamentary majority. When the Minister of Defence von Schleicher failed to draw the Nazis into the cabinet the moment when the Centre could rejoin the government seemed to come very much closer. Papen's wish declared immediately after the election that the Centre would adopt a policy of toleration towards the government found no echo. On the contrary, in the changed parliamentary situation those forces gained the upper hand in the party which aimed at a "total solution", in other words the association of the Nazi Party with political responsibility by its entry into a coalition government.

In August, 1932, discussions began with the Nazis with the object of exploring their aims. These discussions have been much criticised and their course is more or less clear today. It was hoped that parliamentary co-operation with the Nazis would have a settling and steadying effect on the internal situation and at the same time prevent the Nazis movement from growing stronger.

The conversations between partners of such different outlook and aims became a source of anxiety to Papen's cabinet and to the German Nationalists. In his concern over the possibility of a parliamentary understanding Reich Chancellor von Papen began to work for a dissolution of the recently elected Reichstag and this took place on 12th September. The discussions had so far proved inconclusive and now they had to be adjourned with the "strong differences of principle" of which Goebbels spoke still much in evidence.

The position of the Centre still lay between the fronts. The elections of 6th November, 1932, gave the party seventy mandates in the Reichstag, while those of the National Socialists dropped from 230 to 106. According to these results a coalition between the two parties was no longer possible. The Centre now called for the appointment of a strong government by the Reich President to include the National Socialists. But Hindenburg firmly refused to appoint Hitler—who would not be satisfied with a ministerial post—as Chancellor.

Hopes that the reverses suffered by the Nazis at the November elections would continue and increase were not only entertained in the Centre Party. But when Reich Chancellor von Schleicher, who had been appointed in early December after Papen's resignation, tried to split the Nazi Party by including its moderate wing under Gregor Strasser in the government the attempt failed owing to conflicts between the parties. The Centre dissociated itself from Schleicher's plans to dissolve the Reichstag and postpone the new elections for a longer period than provided for in the constitution. Schleicher, who in every respect had been unsuccessful as a Chancellor, had to resign on 28th January, 1933, after the Reich President had refused his request to dissolve the Reichstag. Three days later, Hindenburg granted dissolution to Reich Chancellor Adolf Hitler who had been appointed on 30th January on the advice of Hindenburg's advisers.

Last minute attempts by the Centre and the Bavarian People's Party to have a say in the formation of the government came too late. Papen had taken note of their offer to serve in a government headed by himself, but as it did not fit into his own plans he had not even informed Hindenburg that the offer had been made. Thus, though the Centrist leaders had been reluctant to approach Papen at all, their last attempt to influence events had failed at the outset. Two days later began the dreaded domination by a single party and therewith the last phase in the history of the Centre Party.

Annoyance at having no say in the formation of the government was expressed in commentaries by the Centrist press which stated on 31st January that the Party would adopt an "ice cold attitude" to this "government of contradictions". A conference was held on the following day between Hitler, Frick and the

Centrist leaders Kaas and Perlitius to discuss whether the Centre Party would take up an attitude of toleration and on what conditions it would agree to Hitler's "experiment in government". As a basis for negotiation the Centrists asked a number of questions referring to constitutional, social and economic points the most important of which ran : "What assurances can be given by the Reich government that its measures will be kept within the framework of the constitution?"

But that was exactly what Hitler did not want : to keep to the framework of the constitution. He therefore declined to answer the demand for basic guarantees and with the dissolution of parliament obtained on the evening of 31st January and a resolution passed in the cabinet at the same time to demand an Enabling Law of the new Reichstag which was to be elected on 5th March the last bridges for an understanding were destroyed.

This meant fresh battles for the Centre Party and also, as the *Kölnische Volkszeitung* expressed it, a fresh attempt to fire the electors so that a truly national concentration of forces could be created. The *Völkischer Beobachter* was right when it stated on 3rd February that the fronts were more clearly defined than ever and also right, from the Nazi point of view, when it continued that all the bourgeois parties had lost the right to exist and "if only they would acquire some insight into political developments and some political good sense" they would refrain from taking part in the coming elections "at all", which would be the last.

The Centre Party had now to prepare for an electoral campaign of which it knew the results would be of historic significance. During the campaign it declared war on Marxism, liberalism and godlessness and fought a remorseless battle against Reich Minister Hugenberg, while showing a certain reserve towards Hitler. The campaign was characterised by an overestimation of Hugenberg's and Papen's role and an underestimation of Hitler's and suffered increasingly from the effects of state-imposed restrictions.

From the middle of February a wave of National Socialist terror descended on the Centre Party. Bans on speaking, on the publication of newspapers and the holding of meetings multiplied. Dismissals of Centrist officials caused great agitation in the electorate and in the whole Catholic population. Within the party, which looked on this electoral campaign as the heaviest since the time of the *Kulturkampf*, it was realised that the intention of the government was to drive it out of politics. When Brüning intervened in the electoral campaign on 18th February the confidence he enjoyed in the country became apparent. Brüning deplored the blows dealt at the sense of justice, the destruction of the professional civil service, the muzzling of public opinion and the pursuit by the National Socialists of exclusive power. He appealed repeatedly to the Reich President against the acts of violence perpetrated by the state and true to the old Centre programme "For Truth, Freedom and Law" campaigned for an internal reconciliation. Brüning stressed his party's determination to fight for the maintenance of the Weimar Constitution in the sense of a moderate and reasonable democracy: "We intend to fight, but we will not allow ourselves to be suppressed!" In many places he was greeted with tumultuous ovations and calls of: "We want Brüning again!" Prelate Kaas received strong applause when he ended a campaign speech in Dortmund with the sentence: "We have no intention of hauling down our flag." Four weeks later, when the flag of the Centre Party was still waving, Kaas had left Germany.

The Reichstag elections of 5th March gave the Centre seventy-three mandates, which was three mandates more than the elections of November, 1932. This was a considerable success to have achieved in face of the National Socialist terror, but the first joyous commentaries soon gave way to more sober considerations. For in an increased poll the party had, in fact, obtained a slightly smaller percentage of votes. It had indeed, as a party statement declared, emerged "unbroken and internally strengthened" from this election which had been held under "completely abnormal conditions", but it had not been able to prevent the Nazis from capturing votes among the new Catholic electors. Hitler himself, however, had no illusions that he would be able to make further inroads into the supporters of the Centre and the Bavarian People's Party unless—as he stated to the Reich Cabinet on 7th March—the Vatican "dropped both parties". With Papen's help he succeeded in achieving this aim quicker than he could expect. The Centre found itself between two new fronts.

The election results had rendered powerless the political representatives of German Catholicism. Nevertheless, the Centrist leaders had no desire to surrender without more ado the political successes they had painfully achieved in fourteen years or the positions they had won in administration, the press and public life. They had no desire simply to step aside. The National Socialists and their allies the German Nationalists together held over 52 per cent of the seats in the Reichstag. But under the constitution they would require a two-thirds majority in order to pass the Enabling Law which they planned. Unless they were prepared to flout the constitution, this meant that they would need the support of the Centrist deputies. It was on this point that the Centrist leaders believed they could apply pressure and change the course of policy : they intended to make their agreement to the Enabling Law dependent on conditions which would have meant a return to parliamentary orthodoxy.

Negotiations concerning the scope and terms of these conditions took place on 20th and 22nd March between Hitler, Frick and the Centrist leaders Kaas, Stegerwald and Hackelsberger. Hitler laid great value on the support of the whole Centre Party because, as he said in the Reich Cabinet on 20th March, this support would "strengthen (his) prestige abroad". For this reason he was prepared to grant the concessions for which the Centrist leaders asked. In a statement before the Reichstag on 23rd March he unreservedly gave all the guarantees demanded, in some cases quoting literally from the wishes formulated by the Centre on the previous day. These referred, amongst other things, to the safeguarding of Christian influence in education and schools, the irremovability of judges, the cultivation and development of friendly relations with the Holy See, the retention of the Reichstag and the Reichstrat and the maintenance of the rights of the Reich President.

Moreover, the Chancellor's speech contained many more placatory references to Christianity and the nation than could have been expected and under its immediate impact, torn between fear and hope, the Centre fraction discussed whether they should vote for or against the Enabling Bill in the recess after Hitler had spoken.

In view of Hitler's positive promises the majority decided to vote for the bill. In any case there was no longer a genuine alternative. A minority of the fraction under Brüning's leadership tried in vain to persuade the majority to change their mind. After lengthy and at times passionate discussion it was resolved to vote *for* the Enabling Bill "for the sake of the party and its future". There was still confidence in Hindenburg and by granting full powers to the government as a whole and not to Hitler alone it was hoped to prevent further revolutionary measures and save the existence of the party.

At the plenary session of the Reichstag after this dramatic party meeting Prelate Kaas announced the Centre's agreement to the Enabling Bill on the understanding that the legislation which would presumably follow would be drafted in accordance with the statements already made by Hitler. At the division which then took place the seventy-two Centrist deputies who were present voted unanimously for the bill.

The die was cast. The first free parliamentary decision of the fraction since 30th January, 1933, was also its last. With this vote the last chapter in the history of the Centre Party began.

In the words of the *Kölnische Volkszeitung* the Weimar constitution had been finally buried "without a state funeral". In a cabinet sitting on 24th March, Hugenberg congratulated the Reich Chancellor on his "outstanding success". Hitler replied that he was "extremely happy about the situation in Germany" and announced that in the preliminary negotiations with the Centre he had promised that he would "listen to" a committee which was to be kept informed of the legislation the government proposed to pass under its new and absolute powers. He added, however, that this committee was to have no influence whatever on political decisions and would only sit as seemed desirable to the government. Therewith part of the guarantees given to the Centrist leaders was already null and void twenty-four hours later. In fact, the committee only sat twice and then was unable to affect the course of legislation.

By voting for the Enabling Law the Centre had helped to give Hitler a blank cheque to do what he liked. Five days later, on 28th March, the German bishops issued a statement which aroused wide interest. Referring to the promises given by Hitler in his government statement, they now felt able to withdraw their previous "vetoes and warnings" against National Socialism. This statement was taken by many Centrist supporters as confirmation of their "positive attitude towards the new state". Having felt bound, in the battle against Nazism before 1933, to adopt the same attitude as the Church, they now breathed a sigh of relief. Having climbed into the National Socialist ship, they now felt it their duty to help with the steering, though it was realised that this would not be easy.

When Prelate Kaas left Germany for Rome on 7th April, many observers considered that the now leaderless Centre Party had no longer a part to play. New, carefully aimed acts of terrorism by the National Socialists against Centrist deputies and officials also had their effect and Catholic civil servants in general became deeply concerned about their jobs. Meanwhile, the party leaders could find no means of exerting the braking effect which it was hoped the Centre would be able to apply. Having taken an important step towards the erection of a totalitarian state by imposing uniformity on the provinces in March, the Hitler government now set about systematically destroying the democratic parties.

In this enterprise Vice-Chancellor von Papen paid particular attention to the Centre Party which he intended to out-trump by means of a Concordat to be concluded with the Vatican. Since 10th April he had been negotiating in Rome with the Curia which after 1919 had announced its readiness to conclude a treaty with Germany. While outside observers saw the end of the democratic parties approaching and Papen was working hard for a Concordat so as to reconcile the Church with the Third Reich and make the existence of the Centre superfluous, this party was attempting with remarkable vigour to renew itself by means of long overdue reforms. As the Nazis consolidated their power it had no desire to depart silently from the scene of history. But the cracks in the "tower of the Centre Party" became more ominous from day to day; the collapse of the whole could no longer be averted.

As the negotiations for a Concordat neared their end with Prelate Kaas playing a leading role the danger approached that the Centre would fall a victim to this diplomatic agreement. Aware of this possibility, the Centrist supporters looked forward tensely to 5th and 6th May when the leading party members were to meet in Berlin to decide on the reorganisation of the party "as regards structure and personnel". Central to the discussions was a programme speech by Brüning proclaiming the will to survive. The enthusiastic reception of this speech and the unanimous election of Brüning to be the new party chairman were a proof of confidence which the ex-Chancellor could not resist. One resolution proclaimed that the Centre would co-operate with the "political order" as an essential and indispensible service to the German people, stressed the national aims of the party and called for the help of all like-minded friends.

But the last stage in the history of the Centre Party which now began was not dominated by the results of this resolution, or by the dictatorial powers entrusted to the new leader for re-organising the party, but solely by the election of Brüning. The election was widely acclaimed and Brüning's personality seemed a guarantee that new life would be put into the party. Even at that time, Brüning's inadequate political qualifications were con-cealed by a legend which has not entirely disappeared today. There was confidence that the new chairman must have been clear about the party's future when he accepted election as its leader. It was hoped of him that he would add "the combined forces of German Catholicism to the new Germany". In his election a long awaited conversion to the leadership-principle found visible expression. Behind it stood a desperate, last-minute attempt to save the existence of the Centre by imitating the Nazi organisation and setting up an internal party dictator-ship—one which, admittedly, with Brüning was known to be in conscientious hands. As all the leading figures and officials in the party laid down their offices the way seemed clear for a radical reform which was to bring younger men to the fore. In his guiding principles published on 22nd May Brüning em-phasised the value he laid "in these times of stress" on bringing forward young people "with untapped energies who are able to master the particular course of coming events".

But events passed with giant strides over the old parties and disproved all prophecies that Hitler's rule would only last a few weeks. People adjusted themselves as best they could. Many members of the Centre resigned from the party on the grounds that, according to Hitler's assurances and the statements of the bishops, the interests of the Catholic population were not en-dangered and therefore the Catholics no longer required separ-ate political representation. In future, said these people, they did not want to stand aside from the "community of the people" that was being formed. But the new *Volksgemeinschaft* that was being propagated by the state had no need of the Centre Party and at the beginning of June von Papen invited it to dissolve as quickly as possible.

Meanwhile, it was becoming increasingly clear that Brüning had misjudged the driving impulses of the times and that no initiative could be expected from him. An official party declaration of 14th June, couched in very general terms, stated that, through Brüning, the Centre had expressed its readiness to co-operate constructively in building the new Germany and would adhere to this attitude. When, in what form and to whom this "readiness" had been declared was not mentioned.

A new *Kulturkampf* seemed to be approaching when in the second half of June the Hitler government set about destroying the party systematically by terrorisation. There were hate-filled speeches and a new wave of dismissals and arrests began. On 28th June in Stuttgart Goebbels demanded the immediate dissolution of the Centre, which should "shut up shop" at once: the National Socialists, he said, would not watch the "experiments" of this party much longer "with folded arms". The fate of the Centre seemed only to be a matter of hours. Brüning shrouded himself in silence. The Centrist deputy Hackelsberger had repeated discussions with Reich Minister of the Interior Frick on the smoothest way to bring the party into line so that its members would not merely tolerate but joyfully collaborate with the New Order. From these discussions the Centrist leaders hoped a solution would emerge offering the surest means of "fusing the German people into a whole".

The fiction maintained by the Nazi leaders and propaganda that their quarrel was not with the Church, but solely with political Catholicism, was boosted at the beginning of July by a second visit to Rome by Vice-Chancellor von Papen and by the Archbishop of Freiburg, Conrad Gröber. To the Centre Party—which according to the *Frankfurter Zeitung* had slipped into the centre of the political whirlpool—the progress of the Concordat negotiations made early dissolution seem advisable. Further delay, it was thought, might hinder a development which, in the radically altered circumstances, promised a better protection of Catholic interests. When on 2nd July Prelate Kaas telephoned the deputy party chairman Joseph Joos from Rome and asked him: "Haven't you dissolved yourselves yet?" the die was already cast. Numerous deputies and party members had meanwhile been looking for an opportunity to defect, many of them to make their transfer to the brown battalions easier. The Centrist fractions in the town councils began to break up. The Gestapo closed the offices of the *Windthorstbund*, the party's youth movement which remained courageous to the end. The American *Chargé d'Affaires* in Berlin told his government that people were said to be changing sides all over the country. The much quoted, allegedly impregnable "tower" of the Centre Party was shaking in its foundations.

In vain the *Kölnische Zeitung* called on 2nd July for unity in the party to facilitate the impending decision. In a letter of 3rd July to the Mayor of Cologne, Konrad Adenauer, the last chairman of the Centrist fraction in the Prussian *Landtag* spoke of the systematic pressure imposed on the Centre Party and of the "sad business of political liquidation". It was high time to leave the stage to avoid being overtaken by events. It was impossible now to impose conditions in discussions with the Nazis, but those concluded on 3rd July gave hope that the "positive co-operation" of the Centre Party with the "new state" could assume an acceptable form. Nevertheless, the impending abolition of the party caused the greatest surprise and deep disappointment in many circles where a new epoch under Brüning's leadership had been expected. Late on the evening of 5th July it was announced that the party had dissolved itself. The final statement by the Centrist leaders avoided any mention of Hitler or the Nazi state and the final sentence ran:

"In taking leave we remember with respect our great leaders and give sincere thanks to all who have remained faithful to the old flag. In dissolving the present framework of the party we do so firmly determined to continue to serve the people as a whole, faithful to our proud tradition which has always placed the state and the Fatherland above the party. *Heil Deutschland!*"

With the dissolution of the Centre the last of the Weimar parties quietly left the political stage. Just as many contemporary observers deplored the abolition of the multi-party state as felt that it "relieved" and "eased" the political situation. The law promulgated on 14th July which banned the refounding of political parties proved the Centre's gravestone, the party which had been forced to capitulate after—as Theodor Heuss expressed it at the time—it had been "intimidated and spiritually undermined by doubts concerning the possibility of further useful work as a political group".

Although there was no connection between the fall of the Centre Party, its "departure from the scene of political history" —as was stated in the farewell announcement—and the conclusion of the Reich Concordat which took place three days later, in the sense of an inner causality both events proved to be milestones on the path towards the consolidation of National Socialist power. Some time had still to pass before it was realised that unscrupulous criminals were controlling the state and claiming obedience as the "God-given authority". But when the realisation did dawn, among the men and women who drew the consequences and joined the resistance there were not a few former members of the Centre Party and many of them paid for their activities with their lives.

OSSIP K. FLECHTHEIM

The Role of the Communist Party

Professor Ossip K. Flechtheim is a Doctor of Philosophy and a Doctor of Law. He was born in 1909. From 1927 to 1931 he studied law and political science in Freiburg, Paris, Heidelberg, Berlin and Cologne. After two years as a junior barrister he was forbidden to practise on political and "racial" grounds. He emigrated in 1935 and throughout the war taught at various American high-schools. From 1946 to 1947 he assisted the United States Chief Prosecutor for War Crimes in Nürnberg. After a period as guest Professor at the University of Kansas City he became Professor of Political Science at the Free University of Berlin. His publications include works on political science and a book on the German Communist Party in the Weimar Republic.

A false estimate of the Communist Party of Germany has usually been made by its friends as well as by its enemies—and not by mere accident. For obvious reasons the National Socialists, for instance, made a kind of bugbear of the Communist movement and ascribed to the Communists practically all the evils in the world. But the KPD* has also been misrepresented by the Communists themselves. As an example here is a quotation from a brochure emanating from the East German Communist Party and published to mark the thirty-fifth anniversary of the KPD: "The founding of the KPD thirty-five years ago on 30th December, 1918, was a significant event in the history of the German workers' movement and of the whole people. The final break with Social Democracy which occurred on this day crowned the many years' battle of the best representatives of the German proletariat and of the German Left against militarism and imperialistic war, against opportunism and social chauvinism. Therewith the foundation was laid for a Marxist party after the pattern of the Communist Party of the Soviet Union forged by Lenin. The KPD continued the great work of Marx and Engels.... The party was and is the reason, the honour and the conscience of our people. In the course of its thiryt-five-year-old struggle millions of workers have gathered firmly round the party."

We shall see how truth and fantasy are combined here and claims raised which are quite unjustifiable. It is questionable, for a start, whether Marx and Engels (like Rosa Luxemburg and Karl Liebknecht) have not long since fallen victim to a party purge. And the talk of "millions" of workers simply will not stand up to examination.

In contrast to this false estimate made by Communists themselves we shall attempt to give here in roughest outline an historical and sociological analysis of the Communist Party of Germany in the Weimar Republic, examining in particular those factors which explain how the founding and development of the party came about. In the last resort the history of the KPD is

* Kommunistische Partei Deutschlands.

95

not the history of isolated political ideas or individual politicians, neither is it essentially the history of a party apparatus, interesting and important though the in part sensational disclosures about the various illegal and secret services of the KPD may be. Politically the essence of the Communist Party must be sought elsewhere.

We are dealing with a social and political movement which at times acquired the character of a mass movement. But when we try to analyse the Communist Party sociologically as a *movement* we see at once that this movement itself arose from the womb of an older mother-party. In this sense, therefore, the KPD does not represent the institutionalisation of an absolutely new movement, but is rather a daughter-party and a daughter-movement which despite hostility to the mother or father—namely the old Social Democracy—could never quite disown important characteristics of its ancestors. Indeed, just as in the family the daughter—and more often the son—even when they rebel against their father and mother remain influenced throughout their life, though only in a negative sense, by the parent against whom they revolt, so it can be said of the KPD that it never quite got rid of its father- or mother-complex.

Before 1914 three tendencies could be distinguished in the SPD (Social Democratic Party): on the right wing the so-called revisionists, on the left the revolutionary Marxist group and between them the so-called "Marxist Centre" of Bebel and Kautsky. In reality only the numerically small radical left wing was united to some extent. In the middle and on the right there was an activist radical minority; the big majority, on the other hand, only occasionally used a pseudo-Marxist ideology and phraseology for outward effect and this did not at all correspond to its real nature. In fact there was a broad section in the party before 1914 and still more in the trade unions whose primary concern was with social politics. Otherwise it was politically indifferent or conformist—it had no intention of attacking the existing constitution directly. This became apparent on the outbreak of war when the bulk of the SPD under Ebert and Scheidemann came out openly in support of the *status quo* and was prepared to accept the existing system provided one or two minor defects were remedied, such as the Prussian franchise.

While this section of the SPD was "German nationalist" in outlook the others kept more closely to foreign models. On the one hand, Germany had progressed much further on the path to democracy than Tsarist Russia, on the other, in Germany before 1914 the Socialist movement was able to exploit democratic institutions to a much lesser extent than in England. This explains in part why here particularly the different tendencies were so strongly marked, one of them—the radical democratic—turning to the West and the other—the revolutionary Marxist—turning to the East, while the third, the "centrist" tendency, tried to arbitrate between the others and so maintain the unity of the party.

The deep crisis of capitalism which became apparent with the outbreak of the First World War brought tensions to the surface which had hitherto been concealed. The war, the democratisation of the half-absolutist constitutional monarchies, the victory of the Bolshevists in Russia, the dislocation of the international economic structure hastened further differentiation between the great workers' parties, amongst them Social Democracy in Germany. With the watchwords "defence of the Fatherland" and "internal truce" the war revived in an acute form the demand for co-operation with the middle class and complete abandonment of the class war. The democratisation of the monarchies on the one hand, the conquest of power by the Bolshevists in Russia on the other, gave the attitude to be adopted to the democratic state renewed actuality. The general political and economic crisis underlined the close connection of the class war and partial reforms with the revolutionary struggle for power. In the crisis of the war and in the crisis-ridden and unstable post-war republics it became increasingly difficult to *practise* a reformist policy and at the same time to *preach* a revolutionary Marxist ideology. Everything now seemed to point to a single alternative : either one had to abandon the direct struggle for Socialism for the sake of the new democratic republic and become a supporter of the state, even a "conservative", or it was necessary to subordinate everything to the organisation of the social revolution and be ready if need be even to sacrifice parliamentary democracy on the altar of the Bolshevist dictatorship. But democracy without Socialism or Socialism without democracy seemed to be the one alternative which a party like the Social Democrats had never contemplated before 1914,

7—TRTD

symbolising as they did in their very name the synthesis of Socialism *and* democracy.

In retrospect we can see that at that time—in 1918 and the following years—the solution might very well have lain in the direction of realising both Socialism *and* democracy. If the bulk of the Socialist movement had solidly and energetically supported such a policy much might certainly have been achieved in that direction. In this case, too, the unity of the Social Democratic Party might well have been maintained or at least the split into Social Democrats and Communists soon have been healed. On the other hand without a policy aiming for both democracy and Socialism the split in Social Democracy was virtually inevitable and as most Socialists in Germany only saw the alternative Socialism *or* democracy the unity of the party could not be saved. For how could the protagonists of the Bolshevist version of Socialism (who soon began to call themselves Communists) and the supporters of the Weimar brand of democracy, the Social *Democrats* (who increasingly laid the stress on "Democrats"), work together in the same party, particularly in such a typically German party as the SPD where absolute party discipline had always been the supreme law?

Today, after the event, this dilemma is clearly recognised by observers from a variety of Socialist camps. In his book *Die vierzehn Jahre der ersten Deutschen Republik* the right-wing Socialist Friedrich Stampfer states that no passionate determination was evident among the Social Democrats of the '20's to lead the German people to a new economic and political country. "They lacked the confidence with which they had pioneered in other spheres. Here lies the basic reason for the split in the workers' movement and for its catastrophe in 1933. Because discussion on the building of a Socialist economy never reached firm ground or produced a clear policy it deteriorated into an argument about the formal preliminaries: democracy or dictatorship. And because there was no united workers' movement with a practical and inspiring programme for reshaping the economy the National Socialists were able to use the 'anti-capitalist longing' (Gregor Strasser's phrase) of the dispossessed middle classes and the suffering peasantry as the motive power for a movement which did not strike at capitalism, but destroyed the so-called 'Marxist' parties."

A short but interesting book *Hammer and Anvil* by the

left-wing Socialist Evelyn Anderson, now living in England, offers a similar analysis: "Two workers' parties existing perpetually side by side was in itself merely a sign of the limitations and imperfection of each. Every member of the German workers' movement realised how tragically the movement was weakened by its lack of unity. And yet it seemed quite impossible to overcome the division so long as its original causes remained operative. Each of the two parties saw the weakness of the other through a magnifying glass without finding a way to remove the causes of its own shortcomings. From the standpoint of both parties mutual recriminations seemed justified. . . . That many of the mutual reproaches were justified made it impossible for either party to attract members and sympathisers from the other. Of course, there was a certain ebb and flow between the parties and between 1929 and 1932, as in 1923, the Communists had some gains at the expense of the Social Democrats, but not enough to alter the balance. For the ordinary workers it became increasingly difficult to decide which of the two parties deserved more support. If anything, it was a case of choosing the lesser evil, for the policies of both parties were clearly so hopeless that the choice between them became more a matter of temperament than of conviction." (Obviously one could also refer to other factors here, such as tradition, age or profession.)

It was not an accident that in Germany the cleavage in the years following the First World War went particularly deep. In contrast not only to the old democracies like Britain, but also, for instance, to Austria, Social Democracy in Germany was continually pushed further to the right under the pressure of strong militarist, bureaucratic and feudal traditions and institutions, while at the same time the left wing of the USPD* and the later KPD became so thoroughly bolshevised that they repeatedly tried simply to imitate the successful strategy of rebellion of the Bolshevists in Russia. Undoubtedly the explanation of this polarity partly lies in the historical background of Germany itself. In Prussia particularly the revolutionary democratic forces of freedom have always been considerably weaker than in many countries of the West. Corresponding to the weakness of these liberal, anti-authoritarian elements was the strength of authoritarian, reactionary and bureaucratic institutions, forces and attitudes.

* Independent Social Democratic Party

Eighteenth-century Prussia and the Reich created by Bismarck were military states. They were not totalitarian, but they were "super-states" in which the authorities were always ready to shape every sphere of society with a controlling, protecting or suppressing hand. The pillars of this society, officialdom, the Junkers, heavy industry were authoritarian in attitude and did all they could to preserve the "people"—primarily the Catholic population, the peasantry, but also the workers in their increasing addiction to Social Democracy—in their "religious" faith and still more their faith in the existing régime. Despite all liberal elements the police-state continued into the twentieth century, particularly in Prussia, and this was matched by a kind of ruling society and servile mentality. The so-called "German character" which is continually referred to abroad is certainly not merely a legend. It is not, admittedly, a racial characteristic (something similar can be found outside Germany, for instance in Japan), but it is a typical product of a centuries-old development with long-lasting effects in society and civilisation.

Even before the First World War, the well-known sociologist Robert Michels spoke of the oligarchic tendencies in the mass parties and he also pointed to the fact that military concepts and military language played a great part in the SPD. Later, the trade unions were praised as preparatory schools for the army. In Imperial Germany the workers' movement was dealing with an extremely powerful opponent who kept it down with a policy of pin-pricks without ever confronting it with the clear alternative of revolution or destruction. In order to meet this highly organised and disciplined opponent with some prospect of success Social Democracy raised organisation and discipline to the status of a panacea. Thus in the battle against the existing authorities it became itself increasingly authoritarian. Indeed, the doctrinairism so typical of the German parties made party discipline and unity an integral part of ideology; the existence of opposing tendencies within one party increasingly became a stumbling-block. In Germany after 1914, as distinct from Austria, the enforcement of party unity at any price was to become a considerable factor in permanently splitting the party.

The authoritarian trend in the SPD was strengthened by the fact that, despite their honest demands for freedom, the people in the party were themselves influenced by the formation of character in the patriarchal family, in the authoritarian school and state church, in the autocratic army and in the factories which were still organised on strongly hierarchic lines. Having been taught there that obedience and discipline were the prime necessities of life it was only too natural that they found it difficult to abandon these attitudes in their own organisations. The majority were only too ready to transfer their docility from the old authorities to the new ones at the first opportunity.

Since the failure of the last great revolution in 1848, thoughts of a revolutionary upheaval, in the style, for instance, of the French Revolution, had faded steadily into the background. Since the death of Engels and Wilhelm Liebknecht neither Kautsky nor Bernstein and still less Ebert or Scheidemann had been able to picture historical developments in terms of "Revolution", "rebellion", "freedom" or "individualism". The strength of Prussia and Germany both materially and in ideas in the period when large-scale capitalism and imperialism were developing seemed to prove once for all that the only possible strategy was one of compromise with the existing forces : therefore not revolt, rebellion, chaos and anarchy, but reform, compromise, order and authority.

The conservatism of Social Democracy reached its peak in the internal truce policy of 1914 and the coalition policy of 1919. Faced with the strength of the reaction, the SPD increasingly shunned an open battle. Lacking a genuine consciousness of their own power, the Social Democrat leaders in particular were inclined to picture the reaction in rosy colours, nourishing the illusion that it would prove reasonable and conclude an honest compromise with the SPD and the new order, particularly if the party behaved with modesty and caution. Moreover, to the right of Social Democracy in the bourgeoisie there were few *really* reliable and powerful forces which could help it to disarm the reaction and carry through the democratic revolution to an end. In consequence the function played in England, for instance, by the Liberal or even the Conservative Party had more or less to be taken over in the Germany of the Weimar Republic by the Social Democrats themselves. But this meant that the SPD which had set out to defend the conservative republic against extreme reaction as well as against assault from the left repeatedly faced the dilemma of defending the conservative republic in alliance with the reaction, thereby also defending the strongholds of the counter-revolution in the economy, the administration, justice, the army and education which the reaction itself could have maintained, even after 1918.

This identification of Social Democracy with a democracy that was not firmly established and itself contained reactionary elements was bound to repel and aggravate the left wing of the party. This negative effect was all the stronger in that at a very early stage the left wing had begun to identify itself with the idea and reality of the Russian October Revolution of 1917 and of Bolshevism. The unparalleled victory of the Bolshevists led to the Communist Left crystallising out in a largely spontaneous process and sooner or later this would probably have led to a split even without the intervention of the Bolshevists. But their intervention hastened the split.

The deeper reasons for the split lay in the typical Communist ideology. This mirrors both the dilemma of the reformist pre-war and post-war movement in the struggle for Socialism and also the success of Bolshevism in Russia. The antagonism of "monopoly capitalism" and "Socialism", of "bourgeoisie" and "proletariat", of bourgeois dictatorship" and "proletarian dictatorship" already belonged to the creed of the revolutionary left wing of Social Democracy before 1918, just as did the belief taken over from the Communists in the crises inseparable from capitalist development and in the inevitability of a revolutionary transition to Socialism.

New, on the other hand, was the enshrinement as absolutes of the characteristics of the Russian revolution and of the Soviet Union which at least in part had been caused by the peculiar "backwardness" of Russia : the centralised bureaucratic structure of the Russian Communist Party, the extraordinarily violent and bloody course of the revolution, the revolutionary spontaneity of the peasant movement, the weakness of the middle class, the hegemony of the Bolshevist Party as compared with the Soviets, but above all the formation of a totalitarian party rule under Stalin. The typical Russian influences helped considerably to strengthen the dogmatic-totalitarian and to supplant the democratic-humanistic aspects of Communist ideology. In the course of this process the thesis of the infallibility of the Communist Party finally became the essence of the new ideology. The further existence and development of the Communist movement thus became sustained by a dogma that can really only be compared with the total and absolute claims raised by an autocratic and dogmatic church—a comparison which has often been drawn. Of course, this hardening of dogma increasingly widened the rift between the Communist movement and organisation on the one hand and all the other Socialist groups, the radical-revolutionary as well as the reformist. The KPD thus became a party whose primary aim was to realise its own claim to power and to shape all other trends in the Socialist movement after its own pattern and subordinate them to itself.

In the course of the KPD's history the totalitarian claim of the party became ever stronger. It determined also the nature of internal controversies which always concerned the relationship with other Socialist organisations and parties and these repeatedly resulted in the exclusion and finally expulsion from the party of all those Communists who were even tempted to recognise the independence of other Socialist ideologies and organisations. Here lies the significance of the numerous controversies which went on within the party and were so difficult for the outsider to comprehend. Communists are fond of talking of a firm and clear "general line", but in reality this line represents a zig-zag. Communist parties swung repeatedly between a more moderate course to the right and a more extreme course to the left and in this perpetual swing the pendulum went ever further. Democracy within the party, which was originally far-reaching, was whittled away. This constriction of movement within the KPD became evident when first the left wing and then the right was abolished. None of the later swings of the pendulum—not even those to the right—led to a revival of interior party democracy. On the contrary, the more daring and extreme the strategy and tactics of the party leadership, the more bureaucratic and authoritarian the party régime.

In the 1920's and '30's the Communist parties found it easier and preferable to swing left rather than right. The swings to the right were intended to improve relations with the other workers' organisations, in particular with the Social Democratic parties and trade unions, but they aroused the fear that, despite all assurances to the contrary, they might in the last resort lead to the liquidation of the Communist parties as separate organisations. So long as spontaneous political convictions still existed in the KPD, all attempts of this kind therefore met with strong opposition within the Communist ranks from the more or less left-wing groups. Swings to the left, on the other hand, which confirmed the dogma of an infallible and irreplaceable Communist Party, always seemed like a hark-back to the true character of a "class-conscious" policy. Every truly independent left-wing group soon fell under suspicion, however, for raising too many objections to the opportunism of the Moscow policy.

The liquidation of all rightist and leftist "deviations" and "fractions" passed as proof of the genuinely Bolshevist character of the KPD. The leadership in Moscow—and that meant Stalin, the leader of the world proletariat—was in the last resort the sole policy-maker for all Communist parties. But it was important to consolidate their power and in the choice of tactics they were allowed the widest freedom. In the course of this development in the Kremlin from Marx to Machiavelli extreme dogmatism could go hand in hand with the utmost opportunism. Free discussion, on the other hand, and mutual tolerance of differing opinions was viewed increasingly as the most deadly danger to the Bolshevised and Stalinised party. To the extent that the Communist parties shaped their policy ever more closely on the instructions emanating from Moscow they could, in fact, operate as a unified and disciplined whole. But the price which they had to pay for this was a high one: from living movements they stiffened into conformist totalitarian organisations. It is not surprising that the political quality and human stature of their leaders sank continually after 1918, though in Rosa Luxemburg, Karl Liebknecht and Clara Zetkin the young KPD at first possessed personalities of note who were still deeply rooted in the great tradition of the nineteenth-century workers' movement.

We will now briefly trace the development of the KPD after 1918. It was not until after the November Revolution that the Spartacus League—a small élite of intellectuals and workers founded by Liebknecht and Luxemburg—cut adrift from the USPD. The KPD was founded as an independent party at the end of 1918. At the very first party conference the left wing, which lived only for the direct victory of the Socialist revolution, triumphed over its own leaders: opposed by Rosa Luxemburg and Karl Liebknecht the majority declined to take part in the elections to the National Assembly. In the first few months after the assassination of its leaders, the left wing determined the course of the party. This course led from defeat to defeat, without, however, the party simply collapsing as an organisation. The revolutionary crisis affecting the whole of society was so profound that the KPD continually received fresh support. Then in 1919, the right wing under the brilliant but egocentric Paul Levi managed to bring about a swing to the right and this led to the secession of the ultra-leftist syndicalist wing which then organised itself as an independent Communist Workers' Party and soon after lost all influence.

Though the new rightist policy of the KPD weakened it organisationally it simplified fusion with the left wing of the Independent Social Democrats who as a mass party were at that time a more important factor than the very small KPD and it is only from the date of this fusion in 1920 that we can really speak of a mass Communist Party in Germany. This new party with almost 400,000 members, thirty-three daily newspapers, strong positions in the trade unions and several parliamentary fractions at first achieved certain successes with a united front policy skilfully introduced by Paul Levi. But in March, 1921, it went through a terrible crisis when the leftists had their way and organised a revolt in Central Germany which became the party's "battle of the Marne". Once again an immanent leftist tendency in the party had prevailed with an illusory and utopian belief that it was only necessary to advance, raise the revolutionary banner and the masses would follow. But the March catastrophe was so overwhelming that the KPD had no alternative but to perform a fresh swing to the right, this time under partial Russian influence. This new rightist policy, which in 1921 and 1922 coincided with a certain general recovery in Germany and the world and a subsidence of the inflation, was not modified even in 1923 although the inflation then reached its peak and the general as well as the economic situation had deteriorated to the point of disaster.

It was not until the inflation had been overcome that a fresh swing to the left took place at the end of 1923—this time as a really spontaneous reaction by the party members to the "betrayal of the right" which had allegedly failed to risk rebellion during the revolutionary situation. As the leftist course now coincided with the beginning of stabilisation its effects were so disastrous for the party that it soon had to be abandoned. A new and anything but spontaneous course was then adopted under massive pressure from the Russians and this led in 1925 to the exclusion from the party of the left wing under Ruth Fischer, Maslow and others.

The new Central Committee under Thälmann consisted of leftists who had broken with Ruth Fischer and were completely submissive to the Russians and also of moderate supporters of the former central and right-wing groups. The watchword was now "concentration of forces" and its success was allegedly proved by a steady increase in membership which by 1st January, 1926, was stated to have reached 160,000 again. But as the last figures had been announced in 1924 as 150,000 or alternatively 180,000 the real increase cannot be measured!

The new policy amounted to little more than avoiding the "excesses" of the extreme leftists and steering a middle course. These tactics were continued until 1929 and ran parallel with Stalin's policy at that time who was relying on Bucharin and the rightists in his battle against Trotzky and Sinoviev without, however, destroying the possibility of a fresh swing to the left. There were occasional united front actions with the SPD and trade union work was resumed. In this period of general though precarious stability in which wages rose slowly but steadily and unemployment remained below 10 per cent—at least in 1924, 1927 and 1928—even the KPD became relatively stable and "serious-minded". It concentrated on opposition in the parliaments, on the elections, trade union policy and, last not least, on propaganda for the Soviet Union. The KPD now seemed like a new edition of that pre-war brand of Social Democracy which under the leadership of Bebel, Kautsky and others had pursued a Marxist radical policy. Despite its Leninist ideology the KPD now functioned in effect as a relatively "loyal opposition party". Only a new set of circumstances in Germany (or in Russia!) would again change the face of the party and bring the patched but not reconciled conflicts between groups and fractions into the open. But a more critical situation would also reveal the weakness in political organisation which in times of stability had remained concealed behind the relatively impressive façade.

The last change in the party policy was also determined in part by a re-grouping of forces in Russia. Around 1928 or 1929 Stalin broke with the right (Bucharin, Rykov and Tomsky) which had supported him in the battle against Trotzky and Sinoviev. In the new "leftist" phase he forced through the so-called "Socialist construction" in the Soviet Union which was to take place under the Five Year Plan. But the break with Bucharin also led at once to a quarrel with the "rightists" and the so-called "reconcilers" in the Communist International which also had to swing to the left. This, its fourth change of policy, met with less resistance in that it was soon followed by the first symptoms of the world economic crisis. At first it looked as though the Stalinists had gauged the situation more accurately than many Social Democratic and bourgeois economists who had boldly announced that organised capitalism had finally overcome the crisis. On the other hand, the Third International developed the theory that world capitalism had entered on its final crisis. This would automatically drive the masses to the left towards the Communists. The main danger, it was claimed, in this so-called "Third Period" lay in the party lagging behind the rapidly self-radicalising masses. As the bourgeoisie and the Social Democrats were drifting ever further to the right, the difference was thought to be disappearing between Social Democracy, the "old" bourgeois parties and the Fascists. A Fascist united front was said to be forming which now in Germany stretched from Hitler and Ludendorff to the left-wing Social Democrat leaders and the Trotzkyites. This could only be defeated by a proletarian front under purely Communist leadership. In the general misery this front, if it adopted clear revolutionary battle-cries, would necessarily increase in strength and finally be victorious.

This whole Communist reckoning finally proved a fantastic miscalculation. In Germany the masses did not react to the economic crisis by turning unanimously to Communism. The bulk of the middle class and the lower middle class followed the National Socialists—just as did a part of the unemployed, though many did join the KPD. The core of the employed workers clung all the more desperately to the SPD which for its part developed increasing hatred and contempt for the Communists. This ultra-leftist phase of Communism from 1928 and 1929 to 1934 and 1935 has rightly been called the "leap into the abyss". It contributed to the catastrophe of the workers' movement in Germany in 1933 and proved a further heavy blow for the Third International.

If one draws the balance-sheet of this development one is forced to the conclusion that the history of the party from its foundation in 1918 to its downfall in 1933 was definitely the story of its failure. Firstly, the KPD completely failed in its battle with the SPD for the leadership of the German proletariat. Contrary to all expectations it never even succeeded in all those years in winning over a clear majority of the German industrial workers. Precisely the trade unions, so important from the Communist point of view, remained bulwarks of reformism. Even in the crisis winter of 1932 to 1933, the SPD, although already weakened by National Socialism, could still win more votes than the KPD. Communist influence among the non-proletarian workers—office workers and civil servants, small business people and farmers—was negligible.

But apart from this the KPD totally failed to maintain and consolidate the positions it had won in the Weimar Republic. Despite its achievements—hundreds of thousands of members, dozens of newspapers, millions of supporters and hundreds of parliamentary deputies—after the night of the Reichstag fire the party sank to a small band of harried officials and leaderless sympathisers. Despite all theoretical ambivalence to the Weimar democracy which was repeatedly alleged to be no more than the dictatorship of the bourgeoisie and capitalism the KPD itself could finally not evade the fact that the republic offered it certain advantages and positions. Thus the theft of Socialist achievements by the Fascist arch-enemy which occurred at the fall of the the republic represented a terrible defeat for the Communist Party as well, and this it was eventually obliged to admit.

But the KPD also failed in the always present though not always clearly recognised and expressed desire to protect the "working masses" of the country from the social disintegration, economic impoverishment and physical decimation which the defeat of 1933, the victory of National Socialism and the ensuing catastrophic policy which ended in world war entailed.

That the failure of the KPD was no isolated phenomenon, but was matched and completed by the failure of the other democratic forces and institutions, indeed of the republic itself, suggests that objective factors played an important part in the bankruptcy of the KPD. All the same, the defeat of the party cannot be ascribed to these alone. There remains a subjective failure for which the party is answerable to itself and to history. And this failure was not due to the effects of tactics which more or less happened to be false, but was rather the logical consequence of a policy inherent in the nature of the party itself. This hypothesis is supported by the behaviour of the KPD after 1933 and by that of other Communist parties.

The KPD was never organisationally or politically strong enough to be a serious threat to the Weimar Republic. It was never more than just strong enough to serve as bogy and scape-goat for the rightists and National Socialists in their attack on democracy. Through a skilful united-front policy, on the other hand, the Nazi Party succeeded in folding up the left from the right and in dealing the death blow to the republic and democracy under the pretext of fighting Communism and Marx-ism. This is the most important lesson from the otherwise unedifying history of the KPD. But the lesson is still worth taking to heart.

KARL DIETRICH BRACHER

The Technique of the National Socialist Seizure of Power

Professor Karl Dietrich Bracher, born 1922, studied history, philosophy and philology at Tübingen University, where he took his degree, and at Harvard University (U.S.A.). From 1950 to 1958 he was a Head of Department at the Institute of Political Science in Berlin. Since 1959 he has been Professor of Political Science and Contemporary History at the Free University of Berlin and Director of the Seminary for Political Science at Bonn University. Numerous historical publications, including collaboration in a work on the National Socialist seizure of power.

In a brief nineteen months, between 30th January, 1933, and August, 1934, the triumph of National Socialism and an apparently irrevocable totalitarian rule was established in Germany. In fact, the one-party state was completely established after five months, in the summer of 1933. If one compares this with the events which led to totalitarian systems ten years before in Italy and fifteen years before in Russia the difference is striking. Admittedly the Bolshevist seizure of power succeeded hardly less swiftly, but it deliberately took the course of armed violence and it was years before the revolutionary dictatorship of the Soviets was transformed into the totalitarian dictatorship of Stalin. And Italian Fascism, in outline and aims much closer related to National Socialism, did not finally succeed in overcoming the opposition and setting up a one-party dictatorship until after a six-year process of co-ordination, and even then not in the total and exclusive sense that applied to Hitler's "Third Reich". While as *Führer* and Reich Chancellor Hitler both formally and literally held all the power in his hands, beside and above Mussolini the King and the monarchy continued, however small their influence. Certainly in all three cases it was a question of an aggressive minority seizing power and the political methods they used were broadly comparable, in some instances even borrowed from one another: the Communist tactics of revolution undoubtedly played a part as a model in the organisation of the Fascist seizure of power and this influenced the National Socialists. But all the same the differences are considerable.

There are three main methods of explaining this situation: an *historical*, a *sociological* and a *political*. The fact will be referred to that in Russia the revolution took place against the background of an absolutist political structure and an agrarian and feudal society in an "underdeveloped" country; that in "semi-developed" Italy the crisis of transition to an industrial state developed a particular explosive power which parliamentary democracy proved unable to deal with; that Germany, on the other hand, was still confronted with the political and

113

psychological problems of defeat in war and particularly with the internal structural crises of an industrial mass society so highly developed in that country. All three basic approaches which attempt to explain the particular course and success of the National Socialist seizure of power in Germany take these facts into account, but what is important is the varying stress which they lay on the different factors.

1. *An historical, ideological and cultural explanation* particularly widespread abroad and recently taken up again in William Shirer's book makes a sweeping approach and treats the events of 1933 to 1934 as the inevitable consequence of an authoritarian tradition prevailing in German history. Sometimes it goes as far back as Luther, with whom the roots of the German trust in authority are said to originate, or at least to Fichte and the nationalist movement of the nineteenth century. The question how the plunge into barbarism could take place in a highly civilised state like Germany is also answered with a reference to the fateful development of the German national character.

2. The *sociological explanation* attempts to solve the problem with quite different arguments and results. It stresses the importance of the general conditions favourable to the rise of totalitarian movements and the capitulation of the individual created by the class state of an industrial society through the collectivisation of the individual, the complexity of the economic structure and the susceptibility of capitalism to crises. Here, therefore, the stress lies on factors not exclusive to Germany in a situation for which neither individuals nor a particular nation can be made fully responsible. Among these factors is also the complexity and tenseness of international relations which lead to world-wide conflicts and the development of modern weapons which make these conflicts potentially catastrophic.

3. These two approaches both make the appearance of the totalitarian state seem predetermined by an iron chain of cause and effect. But there is a third method and that is *political analysis*. This studies directly the seizure of power in the new conditions of our time, not in isolation, but with continual reference to the results of the historical and sociological approach. Nevertheless, in contrast to the other methods it does concentrate on the concrete and differentiated reality of events. It is based on the view that only a precise examination of the particular technique and tactics employed in the seizure of power can

avoid the danger of semi-accurate generalisations and assign valuable insights among the mass of historical and sociological research to their rightful place. In this sense we attempt in the following to outline the technique of the National Socialist seizure of power.

The key concept which gives us access to the character and course of events from 1933 to 1934 is the contemporary slogan of the *legal revolution*. From the start the National Socialists felt it most important to stress that, though Hitler's accession to power meant the beginning of a revolution, a profound and universal change, the whole process was entirely legal and within the framework of law and constitution.

Through the paradoxical concept of the *legal revolution* two contradictory axioms of political action and behaviour were forcibly brought together. But these tactics of legality with revolutionary aim were in fact more than a propaganda trick and their importance cannot be overestimated. They determined the decisive phases and situations which gave the new-type totalitarian seizure of power its seductive effect and made all resistance on legal, political or even intellectual grounds so difficult and, as some people think, practically impossible.

This also applies to the preparatory stages. The abortive *Putsch* of 1923—and herein lies its lasting significance—had made Hitler realise that a direct attack on the existing order could not succeed. Even in a critical year like 1923, the dominant forces in the state and even in the army had not allowed themselves to be taken by surprise; despite all internal and external difficulties of the republic resistance stretching from the democratic parties to the trade unions had proved too strong to be overcome by a *Putsch*; finally, the very attachment to authority displayed by the middle class and the civil service which gave the Weimar democracy itself so much trouble was a serious obstacle to any attempt at a *coup d'état*. Though the critics and opponents of the republic enjoyed so much sympathy in these circles particularly, it had been shown that adherence to legality and to the values of security and order (if not of freedom) belonged to the traditions of the authoritarian state in Germany. For that reason the revolution of 1918 had not fully developed, for that reason the Kapp *Putsch* of 1920 had failed and for the same reason the year 1923 had been surmounted despite all dictatorial appetites, including the army's and Seeckt's.

The road for the Nazi Party to follow when it had been re-formed after Hitler's imprisonment (1924-25) was thus marked in advance and weak, even hopeless as his position in the frame-work and according to the rules of parliamentary democracy seemed Hitler pursued it unswervingly in face of the impatient revolutionaries in the party and the SA. But the aversion deeply rooted in the German population after the experiences of 1848 and 1918 to an overt revolution opened a new possibility to the tactician of the legal revolution which he finally used : a dicta-torship sponsored by the Reich President. It was a double weak-ness in the Weimar constitution which made this possible.

Firstly, according to learned opinion it did not exclude the possibility (as the Basic Law does) that the substance of the con-stitution might be undermined and destroyed by constitutional means. This is basically what happened after 1930, particularly in 1932, and the process was completed in 1933 with the emer-gency decrees issued after the Reichstag fire and with the Enabl-ing Law. Hitler pointed to this opportunity to destroy the con-stitution by legal means at the Leipzig *Reichswehr* trial in 1930 when he said :

"The constitution prescribes the scene of the battle, but not its aim. We shall join the legal bodies and in this way make our party the decisive factor. Once we possess the constitutional rights we shall then, admittedly, pour the state into the mould which we consider the right one."

And as early as 1928, Goebbels declared even more clearly and cynically in his newspaper *Der Angriff* : "We are entering the Reichstag in order to arm ourselves in the arsenal of demo-cracy with its own weapons. We shall become deputies in the Reichstag in order to paralyse the Weimar mentality with its own support. If democracy is stupid enough to give us free food and tickets to perform this service, that is its own affair. . . . We come as enemies! We come as the wolf breaks into the fold. . . ."

But at this time the Nazi Party was still far from possessing a decisive role in parliament and even at the moment of its greatest expansion in the summer of 1932 it did not hold much more than a third of the parliamentary seats; the legal route by means of a majority party stayed closed to Hitler, particularly as the elections of November, 1932, reflected a clear decline in the National Socialist membership and following.

But precisely here was the second element of weakness in the Weimar constitution and system of government which offered a way out of the apparently insuperable dilemma of the legal policy. This was the possibility of a government appointed by the Reich President even against the will of parliament and the supporters of democracy. The essential fact that emerges from the immense discussion on this subject seems to me that the President's dictatorial powers under the famous or infamous Article 48 of the Weimar constitution, which was originally framed to protect the democratic system against post-war attempts to overthrow it, now achieved the opposite of the desired effect, though admittedly under a Reich President of a different temperament. The formation of the Brüning government in 1930 and of the authoritarian cabinets of Papen and Schleicher in 1932 had already shown that the legal possibility of a government outside or even hostile to parliament was bound to paralyse the Reichstag and the parties : the continual employment of emergency powers gave them an easy escape from political responsibility and also accustomed the public to authoritarian conceptions of government.

The inrush of the world economic crisis with its catastrophic consequences and the legendary fame of the Reich President who was connected with those conceptions quickly turned the possibilities of authoritarian control of democracy into fact. From the confusing plethora of political and personal factors which led to Hitler's chancellorship one only need be stressed here : in the ebb and flow of negotiations Hitler's basic demand remained constant—he, too, as head of a government appointed by the President must be furnished with extraordinary powers under Article 48. It was not as leader of a coalition commanding a majority in parliament, as misleading apologists still suggest, that Hitler—with the stress on "legally"—reached the government, but through this authoritarian breach in the Weimar constitution. On 30th January, 1933, the new Reich Chancellor could look on his formally correct oath on the constitution which he at once began to destroy as a symbol and completion of the successful course of legality. But now the real seizure of power began. Now the tactics of legality had to be combined with the strategy of revolution to form that specific technique which in a short time outwitted, removed and steamrollered all the counter-forces and safeguards in the political, social and intellectual sphere. For this a new charm was needed to spread confusion, deflect opponents and deceive or lead astray Hitler's allies—the official watchword of the *national revolution*.

This was the slogan dominating the decisive development of the *legal revolution* in the first seven weeks of Hitler's presidential government—until its basis was reformed in the Enabling Law on 23rd March, 1933. Since the campaign against the Young Plan in the autumn of 1929 and more particularly since the Harzburg Front two years later it had been Hitler's tactics to find support from industry, the army and the big landowners in a *national opposition* of the right-wing parties. In fact, this alliance with the reactionary right was only a means to acquire strength for the battle with the republic and as soon as it was put under strain it collapsed. But at the turn of the year 1932-33 Hitler was the readier to seize Papen's offer to renew the alliance in that his conservative partners were now prepared to subordinate themselves more fully to a government under Nazi leadership. The result was a last-minute return of the Harzburg Front at a moment of crisis in the Nazi Party when the economic situation was recovering and the Schleicher government was hatching counter-plans. This concealment of the National Socialist aims under a *national revolution* above party lines offered an excellent ideological façade for carrying out the *legal revolution* constitutionally. This was shown in the composition of the government. Only three National Socialists confronted eight conservative ministers who, apart from filling the most important posts, believed they could rely on the Reich President and the army. Outwardly it looked like a coalition cabinet in which National Socialist ambitions could be effectively blocked. As the organiser of the government, Papen spoke triumphantly of having "engaged" Hitler and to a conservative critic he declared: "I have the confidence of Hindenburg. In two months we shall have pushed Hitler squealing into the corner." But in fact it was not the National Socialists, but their partners, the would-be "hemmers" who themselves were hemmed in. Even before this government of *national concentration* took the oath on 30th January Hitler had revealed his preponderance as Reich Chancellor because, unlike his colleagues, he knew what he wanted: when he obtained the renewed dissolution of the Reichstag against Hugenberg's opposition the front of the non-National Socialists in the cabinet was already broken. This was now repeated from one cabinet sitting to the other. Resistance on this level never, in fact, took place, though it was not until later that the National Socialists possessed the majority of cabinet posts.

This was not merely a consequence of the illusions and opportunism with which the German Nationalist partners had entered the alliance, counting on their prestige and their influence in economic, social and military circles. It also followed from the fact that, contrary to all appearances, power was unequally divided in the government as in the political sphere as a whole. It transpired that the possession of the chancellorship and of the Ministry of the Interior in the Reich by Frick and in Prussia by Göring sufficed in practice to carry out the *legal revolution* without the cabinet colleagues and rapidly to turn the *national revolution* into a National Socialist seizure of power. The latter process was facilitated by the fact that the new Defence Minister Blomberg proved particularly susceptible to National Socialist seduction and to their promises to introduce rearmament. Misled by Hitler's assurances regarding religious and national policy, Hindenburg misguidedly gave his approval to a series of emergency decrees under the disastrous Article 48 and during the first four weeks of the government, in February, 1933, these gave the Nazis the power to control public life and direct or suppress almost as they chose.

This did not take place entirely without infringing legality. Thus a decree of 6th February, 1933, which gave Göring practically full control over Prussia openly disregarded the judgement of the State Court in the Prussian conflict of 1932. Also further decrees imposing rigorous restrictions on the press and freedom of assembly and the abolition of basic rights following the Reichstag fire which enabled the "Third Reich" to maintain a permanent state of emergency for the whole twelve years—all this went far beyond previous constitutional practice. But the appearance of legality was preserved in so far as none of the authorities responsible or capable of being employed for the preservation of the constitutional state resisted or raised effective protest against these acts of terrorism—from the Reich President and the army to the ministers, the provincial governments, the parties, the trade unions and the courts. And this was exactly the function which the façade of the *national revolution* was intended to fulfil in those first few weeks. Despite massive experiences to the contrary Hitler's nationalist partners clung to this fiction until in practice they were outmanoeuvred at the end of March and finally in June, 1933. They did this the more willingly—eagerly almost—in that they hoped thereby to avoid the threatened alternative of the Nazis ruling alone. That their attitude in fact brought this about, legally and without any risk for Hitler, was realised too late by allies like Hugenberg and not at all, even today, by accomplices such as Papen.

Thus the bluff of the *legal revolution* only achieved full effect through the second bluff of the *national revolution*. This note was again struck by Hitler in March, 1933, after the Reichstag elections on the 5th of that month had given a parliamentary majority, not to the National Socialists alone, but to the *National Concentration* with the inclusion of the German Nationalists. The newly elected deputies were summoned to the garrison church in Potsdam where Propaganda Minister Goebbels enacted moving scenes over the grave of Frederick the Great in the presence of Hindenburg and the Crown Prince. Two days later, however, the fact that the National Socialists had seized power became plain when an Enabling Law was passed giving the government complete legislative power. Nazi compulsion and terror already rested on the emergency decrees issued after the Reichstag fire. In the Enabling Law the civil service and the courts now found a comforting legal basis for their willing co-operation. As the law had been passed in due and proper form no objection could be raised against this violent and stormy régime, regrettable though many of its excesses might be. At that time, many senior civil servants comforted themselves with the thought that the revolution, inevitable in any case, was proceeding with such splendid legality and they did more than their duty to ensure its success in their own administrative sphere.

But even skilful handling of the fiction of the *legal* and *national revolution* would not have sufficed to make the transition from constitutional state to totalitarian dictatorship so smooth. This required a further instrument in the technique of seizing and exercising power of which Hitler made skilful use: the *dualism* of "state" and "party" which continued even in the one-party state. Contrary to popular opinion, totalitarian rule in no way implies a compact and monolithic, "one-track" system of organisation. Nor is it true that it functions more rationally, with higher efficiency and thanks to its leadership-principle is superior to the complicated pluralism of democracy. Hitler, in fact, did not attempt to fuse party and state completely. In all spheres of public life rival authorities continued or new ones were even created. Instead of the promised reform of the Reich, for instance, the federal state was changed into an inextricable system of satrapies in which three different authorities often claimed precedence: the *Reichsstatthalter* (Reich Governor), the Gauleiter and the Prime Minister. Instead of the administration being simplified, the inflation of the leadership-principle complicated still further the question of who was competent to do what. The consequence was friction, inertia, the multiplication of authorities and this quickly proved not to be the teething troubles of the new system but part of the system itself.

In fact we can see clearly that this was a technique of ruling that was to a great extent consciously applied and it fulfilled an important function during the seizure of power and later. On the one hand it gave trained personnel in every sphere the assurance that the previous system would continue and helped to win them over to the new rulers. As in the case of the *legal revolution*, satisfaction that they had their place in the new system blinded them to the fact that the freedom they enjoyed under this "double-tracking" was only relative and could be withdrawn at any moment and that in decisive questions the *Führer* with his control over the direct means of compulsion and terror always had the last word. As an illustration of this they had only to look at the law and the administration of justice which had been carried over unchanged as a façade while the system of Gestapo, protective arrest and concentration camps developed beside them and beyond their control.

This indicates the second function which this dualism in the structure of government fulfilled, even during the seizure of power. Above the confusion of responsible authorities and channels of command which allowed almost all involved, Nazis and non-Nazis, to nourish their hopes and bound them to the régime stood the *Führer* alone; *he* was the supreme arbiter whose omnipotent position emerged ever more strongly from the rivalries between his underlings, from all the conflicts between state and party, *Wehrmacht* and SA, the economy and the administration; by playing off one against the other and appearing to agree with all he could maintain and increase his own power with no one to gainsay him. Hitler applied this principle of divide and rule, which made all dependent on him, with a skill amounting to virtuosity. Whether this was fully intended or expressed rather the fitful moods of the *Führer* and his movement which stood nearer to chaos than order is not for discussion here. When one considers the grotesquely false assessments of the National Socialist revolution by contemporaries from this particular point of view, however, the effect of this controlled confusion cannot be denied.

These are some of the most important factors which in my opinion gave the National Socialist seizure of power by means of the pseudo-legal *national revolution* its rapid success in the political and also in many other spheres. The conquest even of remote corners of public life and the rapid capitulation, almost without resistance, of famous figures in the business world and political organisations, in the churches and in the arts and sciences is a phenomenon which also belongs to the specific technique of the new-style seizure of power; it rebounded with immense suggestive effect on the political sphere and contributed considerably to the rapid dissolution of the political parties, to the concurrence of the population as a whole and to the impotence of oppositional circles, particularly in the early period.

Some further important facts in the Nazi seizure of power may be noted. In so far as they had not already, like important parts of industry, become allies of the new régime, the great employers' and technical organisations were soon swimming with the tide in the hope that, by so doing, they would help to preserve normality and save if not increase the substance of their own interests under the new régime. Even in the employees' organisations, which were directly threatened, this tendency gained the upper hand after isolated protests. The nominally powerful trade unions also experienced defections and desperate declarations of loyalty were made to the new leaders which culminated in participation in the National Socialist May Day celebrations. But these could not prevent the liquidation of the trade unions on the following day by the absorption of their funds and members into a single "German Labour Front" which compulsorily placed employers and employees under the control of the party and the state, thereby robbing the trade unions of their free development.

By the summer of 1933 the constitutional state had been tricked and bludgeoned out of existence and already lay in ruins. It had put up very little defence, as the sudden collapse of parties and parliaments, of ideologies and standards of value showed. Compared with this, further events may appear of secondary importance. But all was not yet decided at this stage. In dealing with the churches the National Socialist tactics at first promised similar success. Vulnerable Protestantism was included in a *national revolution* which was blasphemously compared to Luther's Reformation or even to the appearance of Christ. The triumphant progress of the strongly encouraged "German Christians" seemed at first as though it would set the seal on the subversion and capitulation of the Evangelical Church. And among the Catholic population as well the conclusion of a Concordat in July, 1933, led to an alarmingly rapid change of heart and according to the pronouncements of church leaders seemed to ensure either self-exclusion from public life or particularly valuable support for the new régime.

There is no doubt that these weaknesses and illusions also facilitated and hastened the process of seizing power. But in the autumn of 1933 came the first turning-point in the attitude of the churches: in the Protestant "Confessing Church" and in stiffening criticism from the Catholic bishops National Socialism encountered for the first time opposition of wide though mostly passive effect and despite arrests and persecution it was unable to break it in its influence on large sections of the population. But since the turn of the year 1933-34 a new danger seemed to threaten the process of consolidation from another side. Already in the summer of 1933 Hitler had emphatically announced the end of the revolution, thereby disappointing the hopes of many of his supporters. The disgruntlement of the SA, main factor in the brutal success of the policy of terror and intimidation, resulted in rumours of a *second revolution* which would finally cast aside the garments of the *legal revolution*.

Events surrounding the blood-bath of 30th June, 1934, when Hitler liquidated the leaders of the SA, are sufficiently well known. But what is important for our purpose is not only the fact that Hitler used this brutal blow to remove finally all possible opposition within the party and also took the opportunity to murder a number of older opponents, but that thereby the alliance of interest with the army could be consolidated into the main foundation of his power. The army's silent participation in the exclusion of the competing SA and its condonement of mass murder made it the accomplice of the Nazi rulers. When the armed forces took the oath of allegiance to Hitler personally on 2nd August the seal was set on this important relationship and it was against this background that, when Hindenburg died on that same day, Hitler was able to invest himself with the office of the departed Reich President. The claim to legality was here expressed in a stage-managed plebiscite which also fitted into the pseudo-democratic framework of the National Socialist seizure of power.

But the summer of 1934 is also important as the culmination of the seizure of power because in these events the true character of the régime was suddenly revealed. Hitler's public assertion of the right to remove his opponents without trial or inquiry, the claims he allowed to be raised that the mass murder was lawful and that he himself represented the supreme law in the new order—all this was incompatible with the *legal revolution* even in its widest interpretation. The terrorism underlying the technique of seizing power and an indication of how the "Third Reich" would in future be ruled were here revealed with all their consequences.

That this was accepted so smoothly at the time seems to confirm the verdicts which we mentioned at the beginning: judgements about the German national character and a baneful historical tradition and references to the helplessness of human beings in face of the collective and technological forces of modern mass-society. In fact, the skilful employment of modern means of communication, the dependence of the individual on the complicated and obscure mechanisms of the specialised state and the attraction for him of men who simplify issues and achieve success all played their part in the German catastrophe of 1933-34. But two qualifications must be made.

That Hitler succeeded so easily in protecting the internal seizure of power from outside interference and then in mobilising Germany for aggression was due to the fact that the other powers were almost as deceived as the German population by his peaceful professions and his apparent readiness for an understanding. The mistaken appeasement policy is almost the counterpart in foreign affairs to the legal revolution. Secondly, it is now clear how unprepared not only the German citizen was, but also modern democracy for this new technique of the creeping seizure of power. Though the view is mistaken that Hitler was the consequence of democracy, in its complexity and susceptibility to crises modern democracy does, in fact, offer the scope and the means for the bloodless intrusion of a totalitarian dictatorship which derives its seductive force to a great extent from the pseudo-legal and pseudo-democratic foundation of its claim to seize and exercise power.

Today our experience and insight makes a repetition of such attempts less probable. But we shall remain vulnerable so long as the political insight of the citizen is not combined with a critical and vigilant attitude to all attempts to interfere with the democratic form of government and the basic rights and freedoms, under whatever catchwords they appear: discussion about a law for a state of emergency belongs in this category. Attempts to justify or extenuate the past which still appear in school books, though certainly understandable, prevent us drawing this necessary lesson from the past. On the other hand the thoughts which Friedrich Meinecke expressed in 1946 in his book *Die deutsche Katastrophe* are still relevant: "It may be objected that power politics and Machiavellian thinking were not confined to Germany, that they were more openly preached with us perhaps, but not more strongly practised. That is certainly true. But the openness, the nakedness, the harshness, the deliberation, the joy in ruthless consequences, the tendency to raise practical issues to matter of ideological principle—that was the specifically German element and, once these purely theoretical thoughts became weapons for men of action, the element that arouses concern for the future."

HELMUT KRAUSNICK

Stages of Co-ordination

Helmut Krausnick, born in 1905, is a Doctor
of Philosophy and studied history, philosophy
and political science at Breslau, Heidelberg
and Berlin. Since 1959 he has been Director
of the Institute for Contemporary History in
Munich and editor of the *Vierteljahrshefte
für Zeitgeschichte*. Publications include
works on Bismarck, Holstein and the military
resistance to Hitler.

Any attempt to define and analyse and not merely to portray the strategy and tactics of the National Socialist revolution encounters many difficulties. The same applies to the dramatic events in the first twenty months after Hitler's assumption of power and to the often less visible but equally drastic changes that took place in the following years up to 1945. Even the Nazi political lawyers became embarrassed when they were called on to explain precisely what had happened on and after 30th January, 1933. Had there been a concentration of all the national forces of the German people, a "national rising" as Hitler himself had said at first and as his allies in the conservative and middle-class nationalist camps at first believed? Had there been a new start or a restart, an *Aufbruch* or an *Umbruch* as the Germans said—terms capable of every conceivable interpretation, from moderate to radical? Or had there been a genuine revolution? The Nazi theoreticians groped around among these concepts without being able to decide finally on any one of them. And the outward picture of events was confusing enough. Hitler, the sworn enemy of the Weimar constitution, had not seized power by a revolutionary act, but had received it from the hands of the Reich President under the maintenance of outward legality; he had sworn the same oath as his predecessors and in the first weeks of his rule could still be looked on as the twenty-first Chancellor of the Weimar state and not as the first *Führer* of the Third Reich. Moreover in its early stage the Nazi rule offered the strange spectacle of brutal terror and overt breaches of the constitution closely accompanied by a studied attempt to proceed legally or at least in a way that could be legalised. And though the National Socialist movement aroused the impression of concentrated revolutionary energy and irresistible revolutionary dynamism it seemed to put nothing in place of what had been overthrown that could serve as basis for a tangible and meaningful new order in politics and society. In interpreting these contradictory phenomena, we would be wrong, however, to pick on any of the concepts mentioned as the only valid one. They all, significantly enough, have some truth in them.

129

The process of concentration—what the Nazis called the "restoration of a unified national will"—and the revolutionary process were confused in outline largely because they carried out the former partly by revolutionary means, while on the other hand the so-called revolutionary reconstruction of state and society went no further in practice than the concentration of forces. For the peculiarity of the National Socialist revolution consisted in the fact that the aim of the party and its leaders was not the realisation of a well-defined and thought out ideology, but the achievement and consolidation of total power. The state, society and the individual were not to be reshaped, renewed or reformed according to any plan, but simply to be subjugated to the will of the Führer. Such a goal certainly called for revolutionary methods and culminated in the totalitarian state just as much as the consistent realisation of an ideology in the full sense of the word—Marxism, for instance or Leninism. But there was a difference and this lay in the fact that the National Socialist state with its varying aims only subjected the political, social and personal sphere to the orders of the party and the *Führer*, and not, like a system of rule based on dogma, to an overriding doctrine as well. Admittedly the changes aimed at by the National Socialists in the distribution of power represented a transference of power and sovereignty which certainly amounted to a revolution. But the revolutionary energy of the movement was of purely negative character and was only capable of removing or subjugating competing sources of power. Certainly it produced practical achievements, but these—like the *Autobahnen*, for instance—were solely of a material kind, whereas the intellectual power to conceive and carry out new structures in state or society was lacking.

The process of National Socialist indoctrination was in the last resort merely destructive, an attempt to eradicate all the ideological, intellectual and religious influences which impeded or thwarted the *Führer's* will. National Socialist schooling aimed primarily to inculcate a new attitude, the attitude of the reliable political fighter. Apart from radical anti-Semitism and nationalism nourished by Social Darwinism, the intellectual arsenal of the Nazi Party was empty and the National Socialist "*Weltanschauung*" upheld with totalitarian intensity was nothing but the fighting morale of the political mercenary who after the victory fastens his helmet yet tighter. In other words, the National

Socialist revolution was an intellectually sterile revolution which only possessed the outward forms of a general mobilisation, which indeed interfered powerfully and painfully in every sphere of life, but aimed merely at showy achievements and not at a creative renewal of state and society.

This basic fact determined the actions of Hitler and his party after 30th January, 1933. Hitler was neither interested nor in a position to suppress all the existing institutions and organisations which he found in state and society and replace them with new original creations. The Nazis had no need, either, to liquidate whole classes after the style of the Russian revolution or to redistribute property; as they lacked any constructive plans of their own they would not have known what to do with creative openings in any case. The National Socialist movement was bound to confine itself to imposing National Socialist or at least docile leaders on all spheres of public life, at the same time enforcing the "leadership principle" developed within the party, according to which political impulses could only travel from the top downwards, from the "leadership which makes sovereign decisions to the blindly trusting mass of the simple party members". For this purpose it sufficed in many cases to change the character of institutions and organisations so that they lost the ability for indepedent decision or action and could be guided by the *"Führer"*. In electrical engineering there is the *Gleichschalter*, or rectifier, which allows current to pass in only one direction and so changes alternating into direct current. With a technical association typical of their mechanistic thought the Nazis called the process which was to prevent a free exchange of thought between leaders and led and permit the *Führer's* will to flow only in a downward direction—*Gleichschaltung*.

It would be wrong, therefore, to imagine this *Gleichschaltung*, which set the plough of the National Socialist revolution very shallow, as a tactical expedient of Hitler's revolutionary strategy imposed by passing considerations. It was indeed the typical means of the Nazi revolutionary tactic, but, as tactical means and strategic goal fused in so exclusively pragmatic a movement, it was also the end purpose of the revolution, indeed it would be only a slight exaggeration to say: *Gleichschaltung was* the revolution. That it is frequently misunderstood as mere tactics is generally speaking due to the fact that both as goal and as method it was uniquely suited to the political situation which confronted Hitler after his assumption of power. To start with, the Nazi Party's freedom of movement was still restricted. On the one hand, the feelings and prerogatives of the Reich President had to be respected and with them those of the middle-class conservative groups and forces in the state which were more closely allied to Hindenburg: the big landowners, the senior civil servants, the nationalist bourgeoisie and, not least, the army. On the other hand, there was a limit to what public opinion would tolerate. The rabid nationalism of wide sections of the German middle class which had persisted for decades, the longing to overcome the apparently permanent economic and political crisis and a weariness of democracy nourished by these and other elements had, however, created an atmosphere in which a sense for the most elementary moral concepts and principles of political order had atrophied amongst a majority of the German people. This majority welcomed or tolerated the concentration of all power in Hitler's hands and the subjugation of state and society to himself. In the opinion of these people, however, he should only change state and society in so far as was necessary to revive national striking power; more drastic interference, changes which would have done more than shift the balance of power in the state would certainly have been felt as Bolshevistic and encountered wide resistance. It was also accepted that the concentration of power could not be achieved without force, without bending and breaking the constitution, but it was expected nevertheless that at least the appearance of a "disciplined" and "orderly" procedure would be preserved: as much revolution as necessary and as much legality as possible. It is obvious how convenient it was to Hitler that basically he himself wanted nothing more than this and that his revolution aimed as it were only at the submission which millions had granted him without being clear about the consequences. And it is equally obvious how practical a revolutionary method was bound to be which in no way shunned terror and open breaches of the constitution where these promised success, but otherwise, where this was sufficient, worked with changes of personnel, legalistic tricks and pseudo-legal manoeuvres.

In the *Gleichschaltung*, or "co-ordination", of the first and most important sphere which Hitler had to subjugate, the sphere of state institutions, he therefore met with hardly any resistance at the decisive points. Made incapable of thought by the nationalistic fervour of the first few months of 1933 and captivated by the seductive watchword of unity, the German people realised dimly or not at all what was happening to them. To start with, Hitler confronted seven main bastions of constitutionalism which opposed him in the exercise of his power : the *constitution*; the *federal structure* of the Reich; the *parliament*; the *Reich President*; the *civil service*; *justice*; and finally the *army*. Of course, Hitler could not hope to co-ordinate all these hostile or elusive factors, at any rate in the initial phase of his rule. But he took the necessary steps to co-ordinate the most important positions immediately after he had described his goal on 1st February, 1933, in sentences which sounded so harmless to many ears : "So the national government will consider it its supreme task to restore the unity of intellect and will to our people. . . . In place of turbulent instincts, this will once again make national discipline the ruler of our lives."

And these were no hollow words. As any far-reaching action was impossible so long as the constitution remained in force, the constitution had first to be outmanoeuvred.

On 4th February, using his powers under the problematical Article 48 of the Weimar Constitution which ten years before had been the means of saving democracy and the republic, the Reich President signed a decree "for the protection of the German people" which under this cynical title made it possible to ban newspapers, periodicals and meetings, in other words already cut deep into the freedom of opinion guaranteed under the constitution. A few weeks later, the death blow was delivered. The Reichstag went up in flames. This, it was alleged, proved that the Communists were planning a *coup d'état* and on the following day, once again invoking Article 48, Hindenburg issued a decree "to ward off Communist acts of violence endangering the state" and "for the protection of people and state". This decree suspended indefinitely all basic rights guaranteed under the Weimar constitution and imposed a permanent state of emergency on the country. With this "basic law" of the Third Reich which remained in force until the capitulation the decisive stage in the consolidation of power was completed. Without being formally abolished, the constitution had now been robbed of one of its most important functions, indeed of its real purpose, namely to protect the individual against interference by the state and to ensure the observance of democratic procedure in normal political controversy. Any person and any political group objectionable to the government could now be silenced or even locked up without the right to protest. One could almost say that with this decree the constitution itself was "co-ordinated" and *gleichgeschaltet*. At the same time, the decree of 28th February opened the possibility of co-ordinating the next bastion of constitutionalism or autonomous political power: the *federal states*. Article 2 decreed that the Reich government could take over police authority in those states where, in the opinion of the Reich government, the necessary measures for the restoration of public order and security had not been taken. A National Socialist author expressed this more drastically when he said that the decree offered a foundation "for proceeding against the opposition of particularist state governments". In other words, it enabled Hitler to bring the state governments under National Socialist influence, including those still composed of representatives from the democratic parties. But the second step which carried further the development started on 28th February was not supplied with a juridical foundation and not clothed in legal form. In the days following the elections of 5th March the National Socialists used their increased poll as a pretext to occupy government and administrative buildings in the states by force and to impose National Socialist commissioners on the state governments and town councils. This undoubtedly was an unconstitutional action amounting to a *coup d'état* and it shows that the methods of "co-ordination" were not confined to pseudo-legal procedures, but could assume an entirely revolutionary character. However, sham legalisation quickly followed the event. After the duped, decimated and intimidated Reichstag had accepted the Enabling Law on 23rd March, the Reich government was in a position to issue on 31st March a "provisional law for the co-ordination of the states"—and here, incidentally, the term *Gleichschaltung* appeared for the first time in official language. The law altered the composition of the state parliaments and decreed that laws approved by the state governments need not accord with the constitutions of the states. On 23rd March, Hitler had declared in the Reichstag that he did not intend to abolish the states, but he added: "The Reich government will, however, take the necessary measures to ensure uniformity of political intention in the Reich and the states."

This "uniformity of intention" had now been achieved. The

parliamentary majority of the "national government" in the Reichstag, consisting of the Nazi Party and the German Nationalist Party, was simply transferred to the states—the Enabling Law had been smuggled into state politics by the back door. A week later, the commissioners appointed to the states were institutionalised as Reich Governors. These men were in almost every case Nazis and they now possessed the legal right to ensure that the states "followed the lines of policy instituted by the Reich Chancellor" and also to appoint and dismiss the members of the governments.

Within three months, the states had been robbed of all their autonomy and the only function left to their highest authorities was to transmit the will of the *Führer*. In the result a typical example of "co-ordination", but in the alternation of terrorism and pseudo-legal procedure the whole process was typical, too.

The co-ordination of the third bulwark of democracy, the *Reichstag*, passed off no less successfully. Aided by the decrees of 4th and particularly of 28th February, the National Socialists had been able to conduct the campaign for the Reichstag elections on 5th March in an atmosphere compounded of nationalistic fervour, revolutionary excitement, intimidation of the electors and brutal persecution of the democratic parties. In view of the terrorism, the result of the elections provided Hitler with a surprisingly small, though pseudo-democratic basis for the next steps. For he had now strengthened his position in parliament to the extent that he could no longer be simply dismissed by the Reich President or defeated by a coalition of parties—a fundamental difference from Brüning, Papen and Schleicher, the leaders of the so-called "Presidential cabinets", and from the first months of his own chancellorship. Moreover, as head of a strong and aggressive private army, the SA, and also as leader of the strongest fraction in the Reichstag Hitler was in practice the sole master in the coalition between the Nazis and the German Nationalists, particularly as the masses looked only to him whereas Hugenberg had no popular support worth mentioning. It was against this background that Hitler tricked and bullied the Reichstag into granting him the Enabling Law which, though not as decisive as the decree of 28th February in consolidating his power, effectively excluded the Reichstag from affairs and marked the beginning of its complete "co-ordination". It was only now that strong pressure and persecution could be loaded on the non-Communist parties to the extent that Hitler deemed necessary for their final suppression. Moreover, the law absolved him from paying the slightest consideration to the German Nationalist fraction in the Reichstag, thereby incidentally reducing Hugenberg to impotence in the cabinet. A few months after the law had been passed, the feeling of helplessness in face of brutal energy and an irresistible tide had grown so strong in the non-National Socialist parties that they vanished silently from the stage. The German Nationalist Party was the first to dissolve itself, on 27th June. The German People's Party and the Bavarian People's Party followed on 4th July and on 5th July the Centre; the Social Democratic Party had been banned on 22nd June, although arrests and confiscations had already destroyed it in practice. Hitler hastened to stabilise the new situation. On 14th July, the Reich Government issued a "law against the formation of new parties" of which paragraph 1 stated laconically: "The only political party existing in Germany is the National Socialist German Workers' Party." The law then threatened any attempt to revive old parties or found new ones with heavy punishments. Thus the Reichstag was finally "co-ordinated" and in the words of a Nazi commentator its only function now was to "express the unity with which the nation follows the *Führer*".

With the co-ordinated parliament ready and able to approve every law submitted to it, even those in flagrant contradiction to the law and the constitution, the indirect "co-ordination" of the machinery of state was in practice completed as well. Moreover a "law for the restoration of the professional civil service" issued on 7th April had already made it possible to co-ordinate the executive directly. The law sanctioned nothing less than a large-scale purge of officials by ordering or threatening the discharge of those individuals "who according to their previous political activity do not offer a guarantee that they will at all times support the national state without reserve". Reliable National Socialists were, of course, appointed in place of the men dismissed, while over those that remained hung continually the threat of dismissal if they were found to be politically unreliable. With this double function the law—which also provided for the dismissal of Jews—represented a very useful instrument of "co-ordination". The "co-ordination" of state governments and parliamentary bodies had ensured that the *Führer's* orders

flowed unimpeded as far as the executive; the new law now ensured that Hitler's instructions were respected and carried out
in the civil service. The same purpose was served in Prussia, for
instance, by the replacement of the existing *Oberpräsidenten* in
the individual provinces by Gauleiters or SA leaders and a
National Socialist writer of the time noted with satisfaction that
local government had also been "purged and placed on a sound
basis". Yet Hitler was later inconvenienced by the fact that the
civil service was not a mere apparatus for carrying out his orders,
whatever they might be, but proved to be an administrative organ
suited to constitutional government. From the Nazi leaders'
point of view, changes in personnel and continual pressure
remained inadequate and provisional devices. Thereafter, therefore, Hitler abandoned the tactics of co-ordination and resolved
to invest more and more sovereign powers in the National Socialist movement itself. Executive organs were developed outside
the control of the state for the sole purpose of carrying out
Hitler's plans according to Hitler's methods. The SS particularly
ousted the official machinery and with its own officials took over
so-called "political tasks" for which state institutions were considered unsuitable. This process resulted, for instance, in the
gradual removal of the police from state control by Himmler and
the founding of a special office, the *Reichssicherheitshauptamt,*
which ultimately organised the entire persecution of the Jews.

Justice was accorded a similar treatment. Here, too, an
energetic start was made with co-ordination, but apart from the
fact that control of legislation already implied indirect co-ordination of the legal system and apart from the fact that the
organisation of Nazi lawyers' associations, of which membership
was in no way voluntary, offered opportunities enough to
influence and intimidate judges and barristers, Hitler even
appointed a special Reich Commissioner for Justice whose task
it was to "co-ordinate justice in the states and renew the system
of law". But the success achieved by the National Socialist lawyer
Dr. Frank lagged far behind Hitler's expectations and the work
of the special courts called into being on 21st March, 1933, to
try all cases of a political character supplied unsatisfactory results
in the eyes of the National Socialists. As early as 23rd March,
Hitler had demanded in the Reichstag that if judges were to be
irremoveable they must adapt their findings to suit the maintenance of society and the sentence first coined by Frank in 1926,

"Law is what serves the people", was promised normative status. But it was only in legislation that it became adopted. The judgements of the courts, on the other hand, frequently failed to correspond to the National Socialist spirit. And even if all the judges had been convinced National Socialists, that did not alter the fact that the principles of law as well as numerous lawyers were against their conversion into mere tools of the *Führer's* varying purposes. Ideological tutelage and massive pressure on the judges led indeed to a deep penetration of National Socialist thought and practice into the administration of justice, but it could not be completely co-ordinated. After all, even an entirely submissive judiciary would have wished to administer the law according to a clear and written code and not to telephonic instructions and even the Nazis could not produce laws fast enough to suit their rapidly changing aims. Hitler soon realised this and his dislike for lawyers who quoted the book to oppose his every desire was deep and genuine—he gave drastic expression to it often enough. Here, too, he finally decided to outflank the law. In practice the police alone dealt increasingly with criminal and political cases, while matters of no political interest were dealt with by normal procedure. During the war, crimes by Jews, Poles and gypsies were even removed from the competence of the courts altogether.

The office of *Reich President* and the *army* confronted Hitler with problems of quite a different kind. He was clever enough to realise that simple "co-ordination" was impossible here. But it would suffice for the time being to persuade the Reich President to tolerate "co-ordination" in state and society, either through his entourage or by skilled personal treatment combined with a pretence that revolutionary National Socialism would be fused with Prussian conservatism. Certainly Hindenburg's feelings had to be considered, but the Imperial Field-Marshal was never far below the surface and deliberate play on his anti-republican sentiments was enough to present his clouded vision with a reassuring picture of events. Thereafter, Hitler could quietly await the old gentleman's demise. This occurred on 2nd August, 1934, and with Hitler's decree combining the office of Chancellor with that of Reich President the seal was set on the "co-ordination" of the entire machinery of state.

The circle was now complete and only the *army* still remained outside it. The leaders of the SA with Chief of Staff Röhm at their head had increasingly urged the co-ordination of the *Reichswehr* with the National Socialist movement, in other words with the SA. Röhm often dreamt of a complete absorption of the army by the SA. Hitler's thoughts were more realistic. He knew that he needed the officers' expertise for rearmament and his foreign and military plans, and he also realised that with its pride and traditional independence of politics the army would not have tolerated co-ordination. But Hitler found it easier to exercise restraint here because, having been trained to abstain from politics, the army would certainly not interfere with his plans. That in Blomberg was a War Minister who supported National Socialism and soon became an enthusiastic admirer of the *"Führer"* was an added piece of luck for Hitler. So the *Reichswehr* not only watched without interfering while all other spheres of public life were co-ordinated, but Blomberg even declared at a meeting of senior officers that it would be "a blessing if the National Socialist movement soon achieved the totality it desired"—whatever he may have meant by that. When the tension between the SA and the *Reichswehr* had reached a pitch which forced Hitler to choose between them he came down heavily on 30th June, 1934, against the SA which had long since become an embarrassment to him. Having been spared "co-ordination", the *Reichswehr* was now completely neutralised and although shortly afterwards, when Hindenburg died, Hitler made the army take an oath of allegiance to him personally for the time being he took no advantage of the possibilities which this opened. It was not until independent thought at the head of the army proved an obstacle to the spread of National Socialism and Hitler needed a willing tool for the realisation of his foreign plans that he took the next step. Though loyal to the government, the Commander-in-Chief of the army, Colonel General von Fritsch, embodied the army's intellectual and moral opposition and early in 1938 Hitler brought about his fall with a trumped-up charge of homosexuality. In place of the War Ministry Hitler then put the *Oberkommando der Wehrmacht* in charge of military affairs, a body of which he took personal charge. The army was now not merely neutralised, but politically and organisationally co-ordinated and the significance of the personal oath to Hitler became apparent. For a long time, however, the army maintained a certain life of its own, stubbornly resisted all attempts at deeper indoctrination and ultimately provided one of the strongest elements in the opposition to Hitler. It was not until after the attempt on Hitler's life on 20th July, 1944, and more or less coinciding with the fall of the régime that the "co-ordination" of the army was formally completed when Himmler and other SS leaders took over the higher military appointments and a system of so-called National Socialist *Führungsoffiziere* was organised. But even this situation was unsatisfactory in Himmler's eyes and in face of threatening catastrophe he still pursued his long-cherished aim of replacing the "unreliable" army by a purely party force, the *"Waffen-SS"*.

In *public life* outside the realm of government Hitler carried out the "co-ordination" of whole spheres by the suppression of important part-institutions and part-organisations. That the trade unions had attempted a kind of self-co-ordination in April, 1933, merely revealed their weakness. On 2nd May, the National Socialists proceeded to abolish the trade unions after the forcible occupation of their headquarters and the confiscation of their funds. Now the way was free to "co-ordinate" the whole sphere of labour. All workers' and employees' organisations were fused into the National Socialist Labour Front and thereby subjected to the state, in other words the *Führer*. The employers' associations and agricultural organisations were also co-ordinated or they co-ordinated themselves. But they did this in varying degrees so that it could not be said that the economy as a whole was yet co-ordinated in the National Socialist sense. Even after the organisation had been created to control it the economy remained autonomous for some time, thanks to the tendency of economic life to develop its own laws and to personal factors, amongst others Reich Economic Minister Schacht who was temporarily indispensable to Hitler for overcoming unemployment and financing rearmament. It was not until 1936, when Hitler finally started economic preparations for war and Göring was put in charge of the Four Year Plan that autonomy in this sphere dwindled increasingly.

The National Socialist movement advanced cautiously in the economic field, but it took strong action with all other organisations which seemed at all capable of independent activity. Youth in particular was soon robbed of all opportunity for free development. Numerous national and evangelical youth associations "co-ordinated" themselves, while the leftist groups were banned at once. But the party was not content with this. In

April, 1933, Baldur von Schirach, who bore the title of Youth Leader of the National Socialist Party, was made chairman of the Reich Committee of German Youth Associations. In June, Hitler appointed him Youth Leader of the Reich. Schirach promptly dissolved the Reich Committee and in the following months the non-National Socialist organisations were either absorbed into the Hitler Youth or were banned. Students were gathered into the National Socialist Students' Association. For a few years more the confessional youth groups continued, though with much interference, their independent life until in December, 1936, the Hitler Youth was declared to be the state youth and the still unsubjugated associations were, as it were, starved out by a ban on double membership. The whole of youth was now "co-ordinated" in a single organisation and firmly in the grip of the National Socialist leaders; it was hoped that a further advantage would accrue from this in that any deficiencies in "co-ordination" could be ironed out by the schools and other educational establishments.

Though in many cases the final stage in the "co-ordination" of public life was not reached until the later 1930's and in some cases only during the war, in July, 1933, Hitler was already able to tell the Reich Governors: "The Party has now become the state. All power lies at the centre. There is no authority left in any separate portion of the Reich. . . ."

But if this concentration of power in the *Führer* and the party was to be maintained—and Hitler had added, "we must prevent the centre of gravity of German life slipping back to individual areas or organisations"—then even complete control of the state and social forces would not suffice. If the individual, despite rigid organisation, was not to refuse obedience to the *Führer* under the influence of religious, moral or intellectual attachments, then the National Socialist Party would have to get the intellectual and moral leadership of the people into its control. Thus when his Propaganda Ministry was set up in March, 1933, Goebbels had stated that its first task was to "bring about a co-ordination between the government and the German people". He added: "We intend to work on the people until they have succumbed to us." And Rosenberg wrote in 1936: "So, presumptuous as we are, we intend to get hold of the whole man. . . ."

The Propaganda Ministry was the first step towards this goal and through his organisation Goebbels started at once to co-ordinate the *radio,* the *press* and *literature.* The radio was a relatively easy prey. It was simply removed from the control of the Post Office and incorporated in the Propaganda Ministry. Goebbels also founded a Reich Chamber of Culture to which all engaged in artistic pursuits had to belong so that exclusion on political grounds amounted to professional ruin. The press, of course, was given special attention. Strictest supervision and control over the publication of news coupled with a law issued in October, 1933, which made the livelihood of editors dependent on their political reliability kept the press firmly in the clutches of the régime. Similarly, by large-scale dismissals and the appointment of reliable National Socialists to key positions, by legally formulated threats and continual ideological pressure, the universities and schools and all spheres of artistic, cultural and pedagogic activity were swamped by the tide of "co-ordination". As the result neither did nor could ever satisfy the party completely the German people were subjected to a system of constant propaganda and ideological schooling to which only the *churches* still offered resistance as organised counter-forces. It was here, however, that Hitler encountered the limitations of his power. As early as 1933, an attempt to co-ordinate the Protestant churches with the help of the "German Christians" failed miserably after initial successes. A similar attempt with the Catholic Church was impossible and Hitler concluded a Concordat with Rome which for him meant little more than a truce. For the party never gave up attacking the positions of both Churches wherever possible. But a general offensive—whether this aimed at "co-ordination" or at destruction of their organisation—had to be postponed until after the war. Hitler had learnt from experience that excessive violence or haste provoked the danger of broader resistance.

In conclusion we can say that, though organisational and political "co-ordination" was far-reaching, on the whole the desired degree of "co-ordination" was never achieved in the intellectual sphere. For, little as this fact excused thoughtless fellow-travellers, it was only a minority which positively embraced the Nazi doctrine or surrendered conscience to the *Führer's* orders. Indeed it was with a revolt of conscience that an élite from all classes and callings reacted to the totalitarian claim of National Socialism.

HANS ROTHFELS

Resistance Begins

Professor Hans Rothfels, born in 1891, has been Professor of Modern History at Tübingen University since 1951. Having been obliged to leave Germany as an opponent of National Socialism in the 1930's he became a Research Fellow at Oxford and thereafter taught at American universities. He is a member of several scientific institutes and publisher of the *Vierteljahrhefte für Zeitgeschichte*. His published works include *The German Opposition to Hitler* (Oswald Wolff, London, 1961).

The subject which I am to discuss in this series follows logically on the last two contributions: the question of early resistance can naturally only refer to the period after the National Socialist seizure of power, whose technique has already been dealt with, and the implication of "early" is that resistance started in the years of peace before 1939. The subject therefore runs parallel and contrary to the stages of *Gleichschaltung,* or imposed uniformity, which were discussed in the last chapter.

We are accustomed to speak of the totalitarian system of National Socialism, its totalitarian methods of rule accompanied by terror and an all-pervading propaganda, its total claim on the bodies and souls of a whole people. And this characterisation is to a great extent justified. But it requires certain fundamental qualifications. One of these refers to the battles for power and position amongst the rulers themselves, battles which Hitler sometimes settled in favour of one side or the other, but which he often allowed to continue, either from an inability to reach a decision or as a means to reinforce his own dominant position, for instance the jealousy between Rosenberg and Goebbels or that between Göring and Ribbentrop. To take a small, very unpolitical but not unsymptomatic example: in the cultural sphere the struggle for power between Rosenberg and Goebbels in the years 1933 to 1934 enabled a group of students in Berlin to show emphatic opposition to the official "folkic" art doctrine and to campaign openly for modern art. Admittedly the campaign ended in suppression, but Goebbels continued to use his superior influence to damage rivals and he was clever enough to have no illusions about the deadly dullness of official literature and the Party press. The result was that the opposition continued to find many means of expression open to it even in the co-ordinated bourgeois press and at an early stage the indirect method of "laying aim" was developed in which a strongly critical attitude was adopted in studies on Cromwell, for instance, or Robespierre or the mass hysteria of the Münster Anabaptists. When in 1935 Adam von Trott zu Solz, who was to become one of the leading men in the conspiracy against Hitler, published a

145

collection of Heinrich von Kleist's works the relevance to contemporary events of the poet's attacks on Napoleon's tyranny was clear enough and Trott's commentary established beyond possibility of misunderstanding that Kleist became a rebel because he saw the "divine destiny" of man trodden in the dust and that he set his hopes on the "sense of uprightness of the individual citizen" who would rise against an immoral and demoralising despotism. If the intellectual resistance could use such bolt-holes as a consequence of rivalries in the highest places, this restriction of total and complete uniformity was repeated in many forms in the middle and lower spheres of public life owing to the overlapping spheres of authority of an inflated government apparatus and conflicts between Party organs, particularly between the Party and the State, which allowed a residue of the old civil service mentality and professional impartiality to continue. There is no doubt that at all levels in the machinery of State taken over by the Nazis, but especially in the technical branches, groups existed from the start in silent but effective opposition which sabotaged the execution of penal measures, enabled intended victims to escape and kept emergency exits open wherever they could. Anyone who was involved in such matters, either personally or through friends and relatives, will recall typical examples, how, for instance, the whole manner of procedure in a government office could change as soon as a supervisor known to be a zealous Party member had left the room or how some minor police official saved someone's life by "forgetting" to note the first-names Israel or Sarah when making the registration imposed by the racial laws.

This leads to the more general question, in what forms resistance was revealed and could be exercised in those early years and what its extent was in the ups and downs of the period. There is a kernel of truth in the assertion occasionally made by Germans that our country—like so many others later—was the first to be "occupied", conquered and ravished by foreign rulers, though the objection is also valid that rape has seldom been accompanied by such frantic rejoicing on the part of the victims. We should, however, rigorously oppose the view still frequently held abroad that resistance did not begin until the war and even then not until it was seen to be lost. In this view resistance is restricted to the attempt by certain sections of the population to escape the threatening catastrophe with no more than a black eye.

Only for this purpose, it is claimed, was the equation between Germans and National Socialists shattered, that monolithic unity which, incidentally, Nazi propaganda always maintained existed.

In face of this assertion and the by no means unprejudiced credence it has found it must again be stressed that as long as there were free elections in Germany the Nazi Party never attracted more than 37 per cent of the votes (in July, 1932) and that even in March, 1933, at the manipulated and hysterical elections which followed the Reichstag fire, it only acheived 44 per cent. And the further question arises, to what degree was imposed uniformity, after it had run through its different stages, in fact achieved, quite apart from the bolt-holes and emergency exits already mentioned. There is, of course, no statistical basis on which to answer this question. Neither the 100 per cent Nazi plebiscites nor the questionnaires of the post-war years in which so many people claimed to have been "in the resistance" supply valid evidence. More interesting and revealing is a discovery made by the American Military Government. When it checked one million applicants for employment in the U.S. Zone it found that in 50 per cent of the cases there was "no evidence of Nazi activity". Even allowing for all imaginable sources of error, this percentage of recognised non-Nazis remains surprisingly high. The evidence suggests that they merged in imperceptible stages into the ranks of the nominal Nazis, the fellow-travellers and the conformists. But equally certain and clear in many cases is the transition from non-Nazi to anti-Nazi. When Mussolini visited Berlin in 1937 and Graf Moltke refused to decorate the windows of his Unter den Linden office in the usual manner, persuading other tenants of the building to refrain also, something more was certainly apparent than "no evidence of Nazi activity" on the house-front.

So this is a first important fact which must be established. From the start or at least once the criminal characteristics of the régime had fully developed, an aloof attitude and refusal to join in outward manifestations was in itself a form of resistance. It was easier for anonymous men and women to maintain it than for those who in some capacity stood in the limelight. Even when unobtrusive, such an attitude was not without danger and it was certainly significant as a sign that wide sections of the population were impervious to indoctrination. It shows a reserve of forces which the active political Resistance could and did count on, once power was struck from the hand of the oppressors. These were people who were not prepared to accept the régime as a permanent state of affairs, even though they could not revolt against the Gestapo with their bare hands, people who, though in many cases they made the indispensable minimum of concessions, were not prepared to depart from the dictates of human decency in the ordinary things of daily life.

From this moral integrity of a silent opposition it was often only a step to more active, though not as yet directly political forms of resistance. Simple human feeling and the irrepressible demands of humanity induced not a few people to give help to the persecuted. There were authentic cases of men and women who found the courage to assist, hide or provide forged papers for their Jewish friends and neighbours. Groups like the Quakers and Protestant as well as Catholic societies carried out widespread relief work. Among the—to all appearances—small number of those who did not shrink from public protest the Dean of St. Hedwig's, Monsignore Bernhard Lichtenberg, may be mentioned. After the pogroms of November, 1938, he prayed himself and called upon the congregations of the Berlin cathedral to pray "for Jews and the inmates of concentration camps".

This leads to the part played by the intellectuals and the Churches in the early forms of Resistance. That the academic world proved wanting in many respects is undeniable. But amongst men of learning, artists and poets there were many praiseworthy exceptions from the start, apart from the emigrés and those who were driven to seek asylum abroad whose flaming protests against the spirit of evil did reach a part of the German public. Among the men and women of the inner emigration, that is, amongst those who held aloof there were many who used the indirect weapons we have described. And in those days people knew how to read between the lines. Thus the novel of kingship by Johann Klepper was a great success in 1937, a novel which apparently dealt with a precursor of the Nazis, the "Führer von Potsdam", but in fact was concerned with a Prussian's responsibility before God. In the same year, Reinhold Schneider's Las Casas vor Karl V had a similar success. Here a Dominican, a contemporary of Columbus, implores the Emperor to end the sufferings of the oppressed Indios (i.e. the Jews). "Lord thy people are sick, let them get well. Break the injustice under which they suffocate." Similarly in Werner Bergengruen's *Der Grosstyrann und das Gericht*, people at odds with National Socialism could read the writing on the wall. In the same year, Ernst Wiechert delivered an address to German youth at Munich University in which he appealed to his audience ". . . not to keep silent when conscience bids you speak, because nothing in the world so eats away the marrow of a man as cowardice".

Resistance based on conscience such as was here demanded was the type of resistance with which religious people were primarily concerned. Members of sects like the Quakers, the Mennonites and particularly the *Ernste Bibelforscher* offered uncompromising passive opposition at an early stage. On the other hand, to start with there was much tendency to compromise among the organised churches of both Confessions. But the increasingly hostile attitude of the régime soon fanned the smouldering conflict into open flame. Apart from the fact that defence against isolated attacks and encroachments became necessary, there broke out the basic conflict of principles of which the Cross and the swastika were the symbols. Then the Catholic bishops and the Confessing Church did not raise their voices merely against Gestapo interference or attempts to disrupt the Churches from within. What they attacked was rather the National Socialist system itself in its essential characteristics: the totalitarian claim with its complete disregard for the sanctity of personal life and its mockery of the most elementary conceptions of law, the reinterpretation of the Christian faith on the basis of racial dogma, the deification of Hitler and the exaltation of the blood-community of the chosen German people.

Once this essential conflict had become clear there was no possibility of evading it. And it was not evaded. A direct line leads from the first declaration of the Pastors' Emergency Union in September, 1933, to the synods of the Confessing Church in Barmen and Dahlem in the spring and autumn of 1934, or on the Catholic side from the sermons of Cardinal Faulhaber on the Old Testament and the pastoral letters of the German bishops to the Papal Encyclical of March, 1937. The tone sharpened in keeping with events. In March, 1935, a manifesto against racial mysticism was read from Protestant pulpits. As a result, 700 clergy were arrested. A memorandum drafted at Whitsun, 1936, by the leaders of the Confessing Church went still further. It stated: "When blood, race, nationality and honour receive the status of eternal values, the Evangelical Church is obliged by the first Commandment to reject this scale of values. When the Aryan man is exalted, God's Word testifies to the sinfulness of all men. When in the framework of National Socialist ideology anti-Semitism is imposed on the Christian obliging him to hate the Jews, for him the Christian commandment of brotherly love remains binding." With the same application of a basically human approach a pastoral letter of the German bishops declared: "We wish to stress particularly that we espouse not only religious and churchly rights, but human rights as such. Without their guarantee the whole structure of Western civilisation must collapse."

All this was not merely preached and proclaimed. In some cases there were popular protest movements, as in the Catholic province of Münster in 1936 when the restoration of the crucifix to school buildings was secured. In particular, resistance was lived by hundreds of pastors and church officials who were removed from their pulpits and their functions or put in prisons or concentration camps. In Dachau alone upwards of 800 Catholic priests and 300 to 400 Evangelical clergy died. A typical case may be recalled, the martyrdom of the Calvinist pastor Paul Schneider. As early as 1933 and 1934 he came into sharp conflict with the German Christians and with a *Kreisleiter* who claimed for a dead member of the Hitler Youth that he had joined a "heavenly Horst Wessel platoon". Arrested, then released but expelled from his parish, he returned to his faithful flock in 1937, which sealed his fate in Buchenwald. In the camp he became a heroic figure. A Catholic priest has testified that despite extreme maltreatment he appealed repeatedly to the conscience of the SS guards and the camp commandant: "I accuse you before the judgement seat of God, I accuse you of the murder of these prisoners."

It can be objected that all this was not political resistance and did not actually endanger the régime. No less a man than Martin Niemöller, who was himself one of the most resolute opponents, has criticised the Church in retrospect for not having worked earlier or more deliberately for the fall of the government. But on balance historical judgement will surely not endorse this view. It was in the nature of things, and this should be no cause for regret, that defence of the Church's own sphere, in other words spiritual protest and maintenance of the purity of the Gospel should come first. Only in this way could a Christian frontal attack on the essence of National Socialism and total opposition to every totalitarian secular claim develop, not only to isolated encroachments on the part of the government, but to its claim to control life in all its aspects. Thus the Bishop of Berlin, Count Preysing, declared in 1937 : "The question at stake is whether an authority exists above all earthly power, the authority of God whose commandments are valid independently of time and place, country and race. Whether the individual human being possesses personal rights which no community and no state may take away from him. Whether human beings in the last resort are and should be free or whether their free choice based on conscience may be prevented or forbidden by the state." Here the move into the political field is clear, also the road to direct political resistance which was trodden by clergymen like Bonhoeffer and Gerstenmaier or the Jesuits Rösch and Delp. An outward rebellion on the part of the Churches could not have been so firmly based on the foundation of faith as were the ethical and religious impulses of a revolt which gradually acquired political content.

Moreover, there was no lack, even in the early years, of an active and more direct political opposition with in part its own philosophic foundations. An outward symptom of it is the number of death sentences carried out : these were only eight from 1930 to 1932, but rose to 534 between 1934 and 1939. Again, in the year 1936 alone, 11,687 people were arrested for illegal Socialist activity and according to a Gestapo report of April, 1939, there were at that time, i.e. before the war and before the mass persecution of foreigners took place, 162,734 persons in "protective arrest", 27,369 people accused of political crimes and 112,432 convicted on the same grounds. Behind these figures lies untold human tragedy, but it must be noted that persecution cannot always be equated with or ascribed to resistance. The régime, as is well known, hounded whole categories of completely unpolitical people, but it also knew where its most active opponents were to be found and it discovered soon enough who the people were who distributed anti-Nazi literature. The earliest and hardest hit were the Communists who at a blow were deprived of almost all their functionaries (nearly 4,000). But they had the advantage of a schooling in revolutionary technique and so created the pattern for the organisation of resistance cells, groups of five which operated independently and without knowledge of one another. But besides the Party cells, spontaneous groups were also formed, such as the one which became active in Berlin in 1933 and consisted of students and young workers. It called itself *Roter Stosstrupp* and until it was uncovered at the end of the year distributed thousands of copies of a hectographed weekly under that title. Another organisation with closer party connections but also largely dependent on young people was the *Internationaler Sozialistischer Kampfbund* which was forcibly dissolved in 1936. But the parties of the centre and the left, Democrats, Centrists and Social Democrats, who before 1933 had been the real defenders of the Republic, also continued the struggle. Sooner or later their leaders had to escape into exile, but they kept in touch with the remains of their parties. The Social Democrats at first transferred their executive to Prague, then to Paris, London and Washington. In Germany itself a group was formed from their supporters, again mostly from the younger generation, which called itself *Neubeginnen* (New Beginning). It disavowed the still widespread hope based on Marxist-revisionist thought that a régime based on force would inevitably collapse from within and stressed the need to create "élite cadres", a firmly cohesive secret organisation which would maintain contact with important groups of industrial employees. This underground work was certainly not ineffective. As late as the spring of 1935 the Nazis' successes at works council elections lagged far behind their hopes and aims. In Saxony trade union observers estimated that they had polled only 50 to 60 per cent of the votes, while 20 to 25 per cent of the voters had abstained and an equal number had voted against the Nazis or spoilt their ballot papers. But in the meantime the "illegal" opponents of the régime were passing through bitter experiences and almost all the "New Beginners" were also forced into exile.

Despite these reverses, secret activity increased sharply in the early years. Germany was flooded with illegal brochures and pamphlets smuggled in through the "frontier secretariats" or printed on secret presses. Every possible trick and stratagem was used to camouflage the propaganda campaign and make the distribution anonymous. But the Gestapo improved its technique and drew the net ever tighter. It was the working population which had to bear the brunt of the counter-attacks. Losses were heavy. In 1934, the *Manchester Guardian* wrote of the "ten thousand unknown heroes". In the following year a new wave of terror began. Observers with experience of undergound party work, like the Austrian Socialist Otto Bauer, agreed that too much rather than too little opposition was active in Germany. Could mass propaganda seriously endanger the Nazi régime, or the theft and concealment of a handful of weapons lead to a change in the situation sufficiently drastic to justify the losses incurred? To provoke or delude the Gestapo may well have had its attractions. But in the last resort these methods proved suicidal. It seemed more important to save the resistance cells in the workers' movement and in the Socialist and Christian trade unions and methodically train new members. So from 1935 on a certain change of tactics took place which began to result in a reduction of overt agitation.

But the will to resist found other channels beyond parties and Confessions which also included the middle class. A striking example was an unusually critical speech which Vice-Chancellor von Papen delivered to students at Marburg University on 17th June, 1934. The speech was written by a Munich lawyer and Young Conservative Edgar J. Jung in whose circle definite plans existed for overthrowing the government, plans in which men of the Right Centre and of the Popular Conservatives like Brüning and Treviranus seem to have participated. Jung himself fell victim to the "Night of the Long Knives", that 30th June that not only swept away the radical wing of the SA but also opponents of the régime of every possible kind. Brüning and Treviranus just managed to escape over the frontier. Amongst those whose lives were preserved was Ewald von Kleist, a descendant of an old Prussian Junker family. He was given shelter by the Nationalist revolutionary Ernst Niekisch, just as Kleist in 1933 had freed this resolute opponent of Hitler's from an SA cellar. Such cross-connections are highly characteristic of the new situation. Besides cells in the trade unions of both tendencies and employees' organisations headed by Leuschner, Jakob Kaiser and Habermann, oppositional groups of men and women were formed from very different camps, either organised on a local basis or round an individual personality, such as Beppo Römer, a swashbuckler from the volunteer corps Oberland who had agreed at an early stage on the necessity of killing Hitler. Through contacts in the Berlin military headquarters and the

Foreign Office the group received regular information about the *Führer's* daily programme, but plans to assassinate him were never put into effect. One of the members of Römer's circle was Nikolaus von Halem, an industrialist who reached the conclusion after 30th June that only force would avail against the "messenger of chaos". Other names, too, in these early centres of resistance point forward to the history of 20th July, 1944. When Schlabrendorff, who had many contacts, returned to Berlin from the provinces in 1938, he noticed a changed picture which has since been confirmed. Whereas formerly the opposition had consisted of a loose mosaic of the forces which had been in the lead before 1933, there was now, though still no firm organisation, an interplay in which these forces were developing. There were numerous circles in existence which were mutually intersecting. The bond which held so many disparate elements together was apparently more their common ethical convictions than social interests. Into this changed picture fitted the founding of the "German Freedom Party" in the years 1937-38. Its first pamphlet stressed the dignity of the human personality as the rallying point for all opponents of the Nazi régime.

Within these intersecting circles Carl Friedrich Goerdeler was a key figure. He had resigned his office as Oberburgermaster of Leipzig in 1936 when he failed to prevent the removal of the Mendelssohn memorial. He then entered the service of Robert Bosch who supplied him with the money and, still more important, with the cover which his journeys and his widespread activity in combating the régime required. His contacts extended practically to all non-Communist groups in the opposition. Many of them had their rallying point in him. He was in close touch with Socialist and trade union leaders, with retired senior civil servants and business men, but also with serving members of the Foreign Office where a strong oppositional group existed round Secretary of State von Weizsäcker. His contacts extended to churchmen and professors, foreign statesmen and foreign friends and in particular to senior German officers, members of the only social structure into which the Party found it hard to infiltrate. At any rate, the Chief of the Army Command until February, 1934, von Hammerstein-Equord, the "red General" as he was called, firmly resisted all such attempts. And whatever the importance of other resistance circles might be, under the Nazi system an unarmed movement held no prospects of success, either in a revolution after the barricade style, or a popular insurrection or in any other form of spontaneous rising, or in a revolution from above, whether started by a conspiracy within the régime or by leading men in society or officialdom. First the chains of the Gestapo and the SS had to be broken. That could only be done by soldiers, though in an action which bore no resemblance to the "Kapp-Putsch". When in 1936 Colonel-General Beck was first approached with the question whether he was prepared to proceed against Hitler he is said to have replied that a change of régime was a matter for civilians, but that if the civil opposition took the initiative, the Army would not be found wanting.

The events of 1938 made this reserve unjustified and so that year saw the first large-scale attempt at combined military and political action which was quite distinct from all previous projects. It was provoked by the revelation of Hitler's will to war which was shown in the most unmistakable form to the Commanders-in-Chief of the three Services and the Foreign Minister in November, 1937, and was later confirmed in the Czech crisis in the summer of 1938. In a series of memoranda addressed to the Commander-in-Chief of the Army, Beck, the Chief of the General Staff, expounded his objections to Hitler's "irrevocable decision" already recorded in writing to launch a war of aggression. In one of them occur the words: "It reveals a lack of calibre and of understanding of his task when at such times a soldier in the highest position sees his duties and obligations only in the limited framework of his military tasks without realising the high responsibilities he bears towards the whole people. Extraordinary times call for extraordinary actions."

In fact the kind of resistance here implied was not to be confined to criticism from the expert's point of view or to purely military obstruction which was at first planned by Beck in the form of a unanimous refusal by Army leaders to co-operate in Hitler's war project. A note for a lecture by Beck dated 16th July also contemplated internal political tensions and a few days later he was even more explicit: the army must not only prepare for a possible war, but also "for an internal conflict which need only take place in Berlin". For this, he wrote, certain tasks should be allotted, and in the same connection he mentioned the names of von Witzleben, the commanding General in Berlin, and Graf Helldorf, the Berlin Police President.

Here obviously lies the starting point for the planning of a *coup d'état* which was continued by Beck's successor, Halder. In particular, the Chief of the General Staff's advisers in the Information and Intelligence Service considered that if the German people were enlightened about the fateful trend which events were clearly taking the spell would be broken which the series of Hitler's successes in foreign policy—the achievement of freedom to re-arm, the occupation of the Rhineland and the *Anschluss* with Austria—had cast upon so many. If it could be shown beyond doubt that the policy of the régime was leading to war, then it would be possible to overthrow the Government. The various resistance groups which had come closer together since 1937 were agreed on these conclusions. They not only resolved to do everything possible to prevent a European war; in Hitler's increasingly obvious threat to peace they saw a uniquely favourable opportunity to secure wide support for a *coup d'état*.

There is no doubt that their analysis of public opinion was correct. In September, not only did the German public, indulging in wishful thinking and without knowledge of inside events, enthusiastically acclaim the British Prime Minister Chamberlain, the man with the umbrella, the "peace-bringer in our time", wherever it caught sight of him. There were other very striking occurrences. When Hitler paraded one of the new panzer divisions through Berlin on 27th September—as a threatening gesture or to test or raise morale—the demonstration was watched in icy silence. Hitler himself experienced a similar response when he showed himself to the people on the balcony of the Reich Chancellery. The usual acclamation did not take place. At the peak of the international tension there were clear signs of an acute crisis of confidence in the régime.

Whether this was fully foreseen by the conspirators remains an open question. At any rate, they counted on a reverse which would either lead to a climb-down and so to the fall of the dictator, or, which was more probable, if he continued on the road to catastrophe would make it possible to arraign him on a charge of war-mongering. Besides the individuals named by Beck and decisive for the control of power in Berlin (von Witzleben and Graf Helldorf), the Area Commandant of Potsdam was won over to the conspiracy. In addition, a panzer division under General Hoepner stood ready in Thuringia to frustrate a possible attempt by the Munich SS Life-Guards to relieve Berlin.

All this made the technical side of the *Putsch* seem adequate. Its weakness lay in the assumption that the Western democracies would oppose Hitler's aggression against Czechoslovakia and thereby make the imminent danger of a general war plain for all to see. But it must be added that everything possible was done to persuade at least Great Britain to act in this way.

This leads to the political side of the action. The initiative in this sphere came partly from the Intelligence and partly from the resistance group in the Wilhelmstrasse. On behalf of the Intelligence Ewald von Kleist, whom we have already mentioned, went to London on 18th August. He had conversations with important English personalities, in particular with Churchill. He stressed that Hitler was resolved on war. The Generals opposing such a course meanwhile needed encouragement from outside. He therefore urged a firm declaration by Britain. If war could be avoided it would be the prelude to the end of the régime. In conversation with Churchill Kleist went further, saying that if the Generals insisted on peace, a new government could be formed within forty-eight hours. Churchill, who was out of office, was prepared at Kleist's suggestion to write him a letter predicting a general blood-bath if Germany made. war, but this did not help much. The Prime Minister had different ideas about the best way to preserve peace and gave none of the desired undertakings.

A second, even more unusual step followed, this time on the initiative of Secretary of State von Weizsäcker in agreement with Beck. The *Chargé d'Affaires* in London, Theo Kordt, received verbal instructions to seek an interview with the British Foreign Minister, Lord Halifax. The interview took place on the night of 7th September, Kordt being admitted to 10 Downing Street through the back entrance. He produced a statement expressly drawn up on behalf of political and military people in Berlin who wanted to employ every means to prevent a war. This document stated that if Hitler's war-mongering were allowed free rein the way for a return to conceptions of honour and decency among European nations would be finally closed. On the other hand, a frank declaration by Britain might prevent war and the National Socialist régime would not survive such a diplomatic defeat. But if Hitler none the less persisted in his war policy Kordt said he was in a position to guarantee that the political and military circles for which he spoke were determined to

attempt a *coup d'état*. His message ended with the clear promise :
"If the desired declaration is made, then the leaders of the army
are ready to proceed against Hitler's policy by force of arms."

While British action was awaited in Berlin military plans were
pursued. Naturally, a setback was experienced when Chamberlain decided to fly on a peace mission to Berchtesgaden. But in
the critical days of Godesberg when Hitler's increased demands
led to a crisis in the negotiations there still seemed a possibility
of striking a blow. Beck had meanwhile been dismissed, but his
successor Halder was perfectly willing to follow the same line
of policy and take action. The Commander-in-Chief, von
Brauchitsch, was now also won over. Orders were prepared for
an action which was to start on the morning of 29th September
and include a separate attack on the Reich Chancellery. Then at
midday on 28th September, the news came that the British and
French Premiers had accepted an invitation to meet at Munich.
It has been stated that this sensational information ran "like
an electric shock" through the circles concerned, and the result
was that the plan collapsed.

It is idle to speculate whether the plan had prospects of
success or what, if it had succeeded, its effect would have been
on the fate of Germany and Europe. But there is no doubt that
the prospects opened were extremely promising in a general sense
and concerned more than purely military spheres. The action was
not planned merely to avert a war which on sober calculation
Germany would most probably lose and might have ended in a
Communist world revolution. Rather it was part of an aim which
sought to pacify Europe and restore human decency to international as well as internal affairs. It was an action undertaken
by officers and civilian officials as a free choice of conscience
and in the most flagrant opposition to their own government.
This was the high point of the early resistance which was to
continue until the outbreak of war in similar, though less
dramatic forms. Together with all the other indications of an
oppositional movement which we have discussed here it strik-
ingly refutes the picture of the Germans as a pliant and obedient
people who were only stirred into revolt by the threat of defeat.
And even bearing in mind the tragic incompleteness of all
attempts to overthrow the Nazi régime, one should not hesitate
to do justice to the scope and seriousness of the early efforts.

EUGEN KOGON

Lessons for Tomorrow

Professor Eugen Kogon, born 1903, studied economics and social sciences at Munich, Florence and Vienna. As a private business-man in Vienna he was arrested by the Gestapo and sent to Buchenwald concentration camp in 1939. After the war took an active part in the movement for European unity. Since 1951, Professor of Political Science at the Technical High-school in Darmstadt.

From the "Road to Dictatorship" as portrayed by nine qualified authors "Lessons for Tomorrow" are to be drawn. That can only be done by analysing the situation of today. Otherwise my essay would only be a contribution to an abstract discussion to which the title might be given : "What does an upright man, and particularly a democrat, do against dictatorship or the danger of it in his own country?" But the title of my essay obviously does not mean this. It means rather a much more direct and practical attempt to examine whether *we,* the citizens of this Federal Republic, can and should learn from the experiences and downfall of the Weimar Republic and incorporate what we have learnt in our own politics so as to exclude the possibility that ever again, let alone tomorrow, the slightest tendency should develop in this country to enter the path of dictatorship, whether of the right or of the left. Therefore I have to compare the constitutional reality of the Federal Republic with the situations in the period 1918 to 1938 as portrayed by the nine previous contributors.

Put in another way, the questions which finally have to be answered are, therefore : now that the general subject of the "Road to Dictatorship" has been examined, does the meaning of the well-known book-title "Bonn is not Weimar" imply that we need have no concern at all, because the vigilance of the Federal Government and the measures it has taken—including those to protect the constitution and the development of the army—are completely adequate? Or is it worthwhile taking a closer look, comparing the situation now, factor by factor, with what it was in the Weimar days, so gaining a more exact and reliable picture? The mere fact that legislation for a state of emergency is a controversial subject in the Federal Republic, being considered by some people a necessary safeguard against dangers from the left while others think it might open the door to right-wing reactionary developments, justifies the treatment of this subject in a concrete manner.

What is it that is so completely different in this Federal

Republic compared with the Weimar state that it cannot possibly be true that the development of the 1920's culminating in Hitler's assumption of power and the devastation of Europe could be repeated, but on an even more terrible scale? First, there is the basic change which has taken place in the structure of society. I will only mention the most striking differences. Three classes which helped to form the character of the Weimar state either do not exist at all in the Federal Republic, or not to a comparable extent.

To start with, there are no big landowners in Germany today who could exert influence through their outlook, their way of life, the character of their interests or their economic and financial difficulties with the political pressures resulting from all this. The camerilla which the *Junkers* with their German Nationalist social connections formed round the President can never be repeated. No restoration of any kind could restore the big East Prussian estates as they once existed in Germany. One need only think for a moment what a revealing effect a single television programme would have about the extinct *Junkers* and their methods of intrigue to realise that this factor in the political development of the Weimar Republic has gone for ever.

Moreover, the power of high finance and of the big industrialists is different today from what it was from 1920 up to the years when the National Socialists were consolidating their power. Nobody can deny that big capital plays a decisive role in the Federal Republic. But the decartelisation of heavy industry as well as all the other measures taken since 1945 have brought about lasting changes of structure and in conjunction with the disappearance of the big landowners and other changes in society —for instance the systematic increase in the power of the trade unions—this makes it much more improbable that backstairs political decisions could again take place of the kind formerly promoted by men like Hugo Stinnes, Emil Kirdorf and Fritz Thyssen.

So we come to the Officers' Corps. Both its composition and its social importance have changed fundamentally compared with social conditions between the two wars. This time, when defeat came there was no army left to provide the official or unofficial basis for new armed forces, and secret rearmament was out of the question. And after 1945, no second General von Seeckt was needed—if such a man had been available—to take over executive power on behalf of a government endangered by revolutionary upheaval and act as temporary dictator with dubious employment of anti-democratic techniques. Even if it had cherished political ambitions to the same degree, the officers' corps of the new army slowly built up ten years later would not have found an opportunity to manoeuvre itself into a commanding position between rival parties, groups and movements. Though it may be criticised, this new officers' corps does not stand above the republic or in secret or open conflict with it and in many important respects it has been internationalised.

Three main social factors which in combination helped to determine the fate of the Weimar Republic thus no longer have the same importance today. The next most important aspect seems to me the general atmosphere of thought and feeling which influenced events in those days and influences them now.

After the ecstasies and agonies of the years 1933 to 1945 the population of the Federal Republic first tried to reorganise its life as best it could and then—took a holiday from history. It was not interested and still today is not interested in the great ideologies. What Kurt Sontheimer has told us in this volume about anti-democratic thought in the Weimar Republic is miles from our present-day thought, all over the country. Youth does not want to hear any romantic, mythical nonsense about the state, either. Both absolutely and compared with the political storm and stress of the 1920's a sobriety of thought prevails today which means that if any of the inflated ideas for national revival —anti-parliamentarian, vitalistic and heavily laden with resentment—should crop up again, they would collapse immediately. There is no violent controversy today in any class of society about the *raison d'être* of the Federal Republic. But in the Weimar period the opposing forces were grouped round differing ideas for the future of Germany : constitutional democracy, Bolshevism, a restoration of the monarchy and finally the "national community of thought and action", as it was called in those days.

As has been obvious for a long time from the attitudes of West German citizens, neither Nationalism nor Communism has the faintest prospect of success in the foreseeable future—as far as Communism is concerned, not even if the party had not been banned. As far as I know, the highest proportion of the poll which it achieved anywhere in the Federal Republic was upwards of 12 per cent in a small place in Hesse; in any large-scale election the Communists would probably fail just as badly as all the splinter-parties have failed in the Federal Republic. In the Weimar Republic and in Prussia, on the other hand, the Communist Party was always a factor which had to be carefully and seriously reckoned with. In the sixth contribution to this volume Ossip Flechtheim has described how important was the role of the Communists in deciding the fate of the first German republic. It seems surprising that in the Federal Republic nationalism plays no greater part than it does, even in its political expression. Its small importance was made clear by the defeat of the *Gesamtdeutsche Partei* at the last elections to the *Bundestag*, not to mention the hopeless situation of the radical nationalists. Not even certain officials of the associations for refugees and displaced persons could—or would—give any encouragement to chauvinism. But this is no climate in which dictatorship or even political unrest could develop.

But even the former authoritarianism of the Germans which nourished the hysteria for leadership of so many people in the Weimar Republic is now on the decline. The individual and collective formation of character, as Flechtheim states, took place in the "patriarchal family, in the authoritarian school and state church, in the autocratic army and in the factories which were still organised on strongly hierarchic lines". But do any of these conditions apply today? The civil service is no longer exempt from criticism; its social and political standing, though still justifiably high, is not nearly as high as it used to be. Here as elsewhere, moreover, National Socialism contributed to the general debasement of values. And no one in the republic today is afraid to criticise judges, their judgements or their past.

After this brief glance at changes in the social structure and in the political climate, let us turn to constitutional differences.

The Basic Law has created the new German federalism at the demand of the Western occupying powers, striking a compromise between French particularist wishes, the British practice of decentralisation and American pragmatism. The new federalism has been much criticised by many people for the delays and inefficiency it entails, but no one can deny that in the regions it protects it has contributed to creating sound conditions of autonomy which are anything but favourable to the revival of dictatorial aims. Bavaria had special importance in the rise of

National Socialism. Today the special political position of Bavaria has changed because the over-powerful State of Prussia no longer exists. When the Social Democrats and the Centrists in this "republican stronghold" capitulated on 20th July, 1932, to Franz von Papen's *coup d'état*, Joseph Goebbels wrote in his diary: "The Reds have missed their big chance. It will never recur." As far as the states are concerned a fateful crisis like this could never arise—North Rhine-Westphalia, our largest state, has no sort of relationship to the others comparable to that of Prussia in the Weimar Republic. Politically, of course, regionalism "Swissifies" us considerably, but as far as relapses into former tendencies are concerned that can only be useful.

And we should remember what Ernst Fraenkel has said in his contribution to this volume about two further important differences between the Weimar constitution and the present one: "With the aim of preventing a renewed failure of the parliamentary system of government the Basic Law has restricted the budgetary supremacy of the *Bundestag* and the *Bundesrat* and modified the vote of censure, thereby watering down the basic principles of what hitherto has been considered in Germany as the inalienable characteristic of parliamentarianism. According to Article 113 of the Basic Law parliament can only insert new items of expenditure or increase existing ones in the budgetary proposals laid before it if the Federal Government gives its approval; under Article 67 a vote of no confidence can only be passed on the Federal Chancellor if a majority of the *Bundestag* at the same time elects his successor. Revolutionary though these provisions may seem to the European theoretician of parliamentarianism whose thought follows abstract and dogmatic paths, they, or at least their underlying principles, are perfectly well known to the student of English constitutional practice. The constitutional departures of the Basic Law from the Weimar constitution largely represent a closer approximation to the model of English parliamentarianism which in more than one respect was grossly misunderstood in 1919." The so-called "Chancellor-democracy" which resulted from this has made provision for the use of emergency powers superfluous in our constitution—the "authoritarian breach in the Weimar constitution", as Karl Dietrich Bracher called the old Article 48 in his contribution to this volume.

That we have been spared the multi-party state which

contributed decisively to the plebiscitary development in the Weimar Republic and to its collapse and the frustration of parliamentary business is not due, incidentally, to the character of the Basic Law, but the fact must be stressed in the preceding context because it happily reinforced a trend in national politics which the fathers of our constitution consciously wished to foster. Many circumstances have helped to form a healthy concentration of opinion amongst the electorate, not least the feeling of the people that even in a system of freedom political eccentricities should not be encouraged in difficult times.

International relations have also helped to give our second republic a better start that the first (and incidentally the second has now lasted as long as the first—another reason why comparisons are not out of place). The unconditional surrender on 8th May, 1945, with the consequent lack of any state authority of our own, in other words, the occupation régime prevented revolutionary situations and crises arising in which once again a German government would have had to struggle to survive, and again with doubtful success. After the first phase of attempted reparation with the dismantling of plant which it entailed (later to prove a relative advantage when it came to rebuilding our industries), the Western allies avoided repeating the mistake of the 1920's and demanding gigantic reparations deliveries from current production. Indeed, like all other countries which made use of it, we were allowed the full benefit of Marshall Plan assistance so that after the currency reform had taken place in 1948 the new republic could arise on a solid economic foundation. And within the world-embracing conflict between the systems of the leading powers, just as the German Democratic Repubilc was called into being and organised on the other side, so the Federal Republic became almost at once an equal partner in the arrangements for a Western alliance, thus making the problem of revision such as always arises from the condition of the conquered in post-war situations of far less importance than after the First World War.

As a consequence of the totally different circumstances almost every German question of importance, when it arose, was always internationalised or at least Europeanised and none had a dangerous, enclosed and purely national area of incubation. Though democracy after the Western pattern was for a second time demanded of the German people—in this case in the

American, British and French occupation zones—as it were as a burden arising from the war, in this greatest disaster in German history reason had a much better chance of gaining the upper hand from the start than after 1918.

The initial conditions for a liberal régime in Germany armed with all the social, economic and cultural advantages expected of a modern democracy were therefore good. The experience of more than twelve years has shown that the foundations which were laid cannot be called faulty. What, therefore, is the reason for the unease which many people feel when they ask themselves seriously how long our provisional State can last? Many causes for concern emerge without any reference to Weimar if we examine the Bonn State with friendly but unprejudiced eyes. This examination will reveal where the neuralgic points lie and the "lessons for tomorrow" to be derived from previous chapters will also apply to them.

It is almost entirely a question of negative possibilities, of the reverse side of proven and clearly apparent advantages. And here, too, is a difference from Weimar : in those days the prevailing evil, a product of circumstances and of the spirit of the times, was from the start a big factor in itself, clearly recognisable in several political personages and movements, and a factor that had to be reckoned with even though it changed form and colour through the years: the will to total power. As we have seen, this will then prevailed in the National Socialist manner, partly by legal means and partly by force. But if crises developed in our democracy today they would have to spring from circumstances alone.

So we must examine the reverse side of these proven advantages. Amongst the latter our capacity for hard work springs to mind which found its outlet on 20th June, 1948, when a currency reform took place of purely technical scope without reference to the prevailing distribution of property. To universal admiration, the start under the general motto "Enrich yourselves . . . and show what you can do" released only three years after the total collapse of a total war effort enormous new energies in all sections of the German population. Almost everyone had a share in the general prosperity which soon resulted and it was therefore called a "social market-economy", although in reality it was an economically very successful system of unrestricted egoism of the get-rich variety. In this system there has been no opportunity so far to test the most specific quality of a pluralistic democracy : the sense of solidarity arising from the spirit of fundamental human values. Nobody knows, but everyone suspects what would become of us in the event of a severe and persistent economic crisis. This is one reason why a crisis must not be allowed to occur. Fortunately—and this helps the cause of democracy in Germany—the resources of opportunism have become so well developed internationally since the world economic catastrophe of 1929 to 1934 that a danger of this kind need hardly be feared; moreover the Federal Republic is the only highly industrialised country lying on the demarcation line between East and West that runs round the northern hemisphere—in other words, politically it is a frontal area *par excellence* in which the world of the western democracies simply could not afford an economic crisis of the kind described. For this would inevitably result in another catastrophe in which egoism and solidarity would strive for mastery and the end would undoubtedly be war to the knife between social groups and individuals.

The hidden, deep-seated, well-founded fear of any noticeable change in the conditions on which our economic prosperity rests is the true, though illegitimate parent of the political formula "No experiments!" This conceals the fact that, much as we are sorry for them and gladly though we send them parcels, we have no *confidence in the power of freedom* when we contemplate the Germans on the other side of the Iron Curtain who have been transferred from one dictatorship to another. What Erich Matthias said in his contribution about the Social Democrats and their relationship to power in the Weimar period now applies to the whole people in the Federal Republic: "Their real failure lay in the fact that they had no political plan for themselves either in power or in opposition. Their withdrawal (from the Grand Coalition in 1930) was not the prelude to a new policy but an escape into noisy opposition without tangible aims, an opposition . . . notable for a hopeless lack of constructive initiative and tactical elasticity." Today, in foreign affairs, we call this the "immobilism" of the Federal Republic—this, too, is the reverse side of a medal, in this case of the old German adventurousness. I only mention it to illustrate that nothing has

been proved apart from our economic, technical and organisational efficiency, not even our faith in freedom. This can be
confirmed by many other examples, for instance by the widespread fear of the—alleged—"ideological superiority" of the
eastern dictatorships which is ascribed, suspiciously enough, to
their "simplicity" and "compactness". Is it possible to mistrust
more profoundly the strength of the pluralistic system which
derives from the very versatility and richness of the non-
collectivised individual and non-collectivised groups?

It is in this connection that, despite respectable polls at election
time, the attitude to parliament in the Federal Republic has remained extremely equivocal. In October, 1961, during the performance which the Christian and the Free Democrats staged
in their coalition negotiations against the alarming background
of the Berlin crisis, it became apparent at once and throughout
the country that no major scandal was needed, but only a
noticeable failure on the part of leading democratic politicians
to turn contempt for certain party practices—perfectly healthy
in itself and at times a valuable corrective in a democracy—into
disdain for the system as a whole. Here again the German
tendency appears which Ernst Fraenkel referred to in his contribution to this volume : a tendency to look on politics as the
sphere of philosophical principles and therefore to take a per-
fectionist and doctrinaire approach. It is, of course, unfortunate
when newly elected political representatives with fresh hopes
attached to them give cause to doubt their calibre; nevertheless,
one would feel happier if the citizens of the Federal Republic
accepted the unsatisfactory aspects of a pluralistic system of
freedom with a realistic approach which does not expect more
than a modest level of performance in the difficult business of
politics except when truly historic decisions are involved. But
as things have been with us so far, both as regards the electors and
the elected, the question whether very many people would
support the pluralistic system in a situation of danger would have
to be answered : democracy—yes; parliament—no. But, seen in
the proper light, this shows that democracy is by no means
firmly anchored yet in the Federal Republic. Thinking along
lines of principle, particularly of a juristic kind, and the
championing of interests have not yet become fused in our
country. But on its own neither the one nor the other could
survive a critical situation. Parliament ought to be the place

where they work together in the public eye and as such be familiar to everyone, the central stronghold of democracy.

Dr. Konrad Adenauer, the master of improvisation and *ad hoc* compromise solutions, has a large share of responsibility that this has not yet properly come about. When he took over the office of Federal Chancellor with the famous single vote—his own, as people say—Adenauer proved to be a first-rate politician and as such excellently suited to the situation which he found: one of those situations which at the start and for a good portion of the road required a firm, unerring and authoritative hand. In 1930, Brüning, too, had to strengthen the power of the executive and as Rudolf Morsey has described in his contribution all he tended to demand of the parliamentary parties was non-interference rather than their active co-operation. The situations which provoked such attempted solutions between the two world wars and repeatedly threw up dictatorships of varying kinds have been analysed by Theodor Eschenburg in the first contribution to this volume. But in the special conditions prevailing from 1945 to 1947 it was merely a matter of granting authority within the democracy to the leading politician who distributed his directives. The Basic Law made this possible. Special powers were unnecessary. But Dr. Adenauer *took* them—in his own particular style of governing—and the majority in the *Bundestag* was content. It and the country could afford this attitude without noteworthy harm so long as the foundations had to be laid. So the Federal Chancellor was allowed his own way. It was not his method at all to exclude the parties, but to use them, as far as he could, as parliamentary rubber stamps. It gradually became clear that he was developing his style into a patriarchal and authoritarian system of democracy; he had no intention at all of encouraging independence or partnership. By 1957 at the latest, when the third elections to the *Bundestag* took place and the republic was firmly established as the faithful ally of one side and the even more reliable opponent of the other, provision for a change should have been made in the interest of internal democratic development. Too late—Dr. Adenauer had already ensured that no active revolt was possible in the ranks of his own party. And that is how the situation remained, right up to and beyond the fourth elections, and will remain so long as *he* chooses to stay. There is a certain amount of discontent,

of course, but many people are happy to combine economic
agility with political quietism.

In reference to our theme all this has two unpleasant consequences, amongst others. The government is coming to be
looked on increasingly as a party which has begun to equate itself with the state and which must be preserved as a kind of
heritage. All available means are employed to foster this attitude,
including continual reference to international dangers, although
in the sense implied these belong to the permanent characteristics
of our situation. As a consequence of the desire to turn predominant rule into sole rule there then appears a tendency not
only to sterilise opposition, but to brand it as heretical; from
time to time, whenever it appears desirable on party political
grounds, it is even depicted as a danger to the national life. But
this is a fundamental offence against pluralistic democracy as
such which after all lives on a basis of controversy consisting of
argument and tolerance. When serious efforts are made to rob
a minority of the chance to become a majority democracy ceases
and totalitarianism begins. The ideological mystification of
politics, still much in vogue with us and sometimes deliberately
encouraged, works in the same dangerous direction.

There is all too strong a tendency to use anti-Communism in
its primitive and simplified version as a convenient common
denominator for the numerous attempts to stabilise one's own
predominance in the republic, dogmatise one's own opinions and
stifle opposition even in thought. The danger which such a
practice can represent even for firmly established democracies
was shown in the early 1950's by the case of Senator Joseph
McCarthy in the U.S.A.: a few steps further and the man would
have had enough support to stand perhaps for the Presidency
and perhaps to be elected—the consequences for America and
the world would have been indescribable. That this sort of anti-
Communism also paralyses foreign policy and encourages an
exclusive faith in the methods of armed force and counter-
propaganda is a further reason to treat it as a political cancer.
One must know the opponent as he is, not as one imagines him
to be, from whatever motives.

Under the drum-fire of accusations from the East playing on
western memories of the Nazi occupation of Europe a certain
manifestation of the power politics practised by the Federal

Republic as a consequence of the world political conflict has helped in many places to make our democracy appear somewhat suspect, to put it mildly. Strong and repeated assertions that the Federal Army must be equipped with atomic weapons within the NATO alliance naturally increase suspicion that our government harbours revanchist aims and after systematically extending the armed force at its disposal will suddenly turn to Hitlerian threats. This, of course, is not true in any sense; the defence policy even of our Defence Minister is not governed by the intention of one day serving a policy of revision, let alone of revenge—assuming this would be possible within the Western Alliance, which again is not the case. As the situation has developed the Federal Republic cannot keep itself stripped of all military armaments merely to make a good impression on its eastern neighbour. All the same....

Some qualification is still necessary. If our policy had been more flexible, if it had been searching since Stalin's death for step-by-step changes acceptable to both sides—*our* policy as having a prime interest in this for the sake of Germany—, if it had made diplomatic use of power in the course of its development, if it had had realistic ideas, if it had not so frequently declined discussional contacts our democracy would have established to some extent its reputation and so be better protected perhaps against the doubts to which it is continually exposed.

The objective and critical comment which must be made therefore is that, though they may possess the very best personal intentions, the official protagonists in the Federal Republic of the *policy of strength* as a policy of "nothing but strength" *may be preparing the way for other forces* which in certain circumstances will come after them, sooner or later, whenever it may be—after all, what are twelve years in the history of peoples and states!

This is where the *argument of an impulse from outside* comes in. Though everything speaks against the possibility of totalitarian tendencies within the Federal Republic combining in the foreseeable future to create the danger of dictatorship, it seems not at all impossible that it might arise from the use of force elsewhere. It could only come in the form of *National Bolshevism* if a small, completely disarmed neutrality zone came about in Central Europe within which a few nationalist activists agreed with the Communists on a *coup d'état* and then successfully carried it out—obviously a most improbable combination of circumstances. The assertion maintained in the East and continually disseminated from the East that a combination of revisionist policy and military power in the Federal Republic is only a question of time and opportunity is not convincing either —but the counter-argument of American and Russian atomic super-power overshadowing and controlling all certainly is.

A *Fascist infection* of the Federal Republic by France is a different matter. It would not be impossible either if the policy of the Algerian French and the whole of their OAS supporters prevailed against de Gaulle during or after the end of his rule, or in the event of the Popular Front policy forestalling them. Certain privileged circles in Germany would be so roused by one development and against the other that they might be tempted to steer our politics into pre-Fascist channels and many worthy people in the country would find reasons enough to welcome this as clearly necessary. Contacts with the forces which had triumphed in France would be numerous and, ironically enough, the organisations for European co-operation which have developed friendly relations but have not been supplied with a protective supranational authority would facilitate them.

In view of such a possibility—no doubt Italy would be quickly drawn into the wake of the decision for the radical right or the radical left—present attempts in the Federal Republic to produce *legislation for an emergency* are of special importance. To provide against the danger of *coups d'état* it is completely unnecessary; who could actualise such a danger? Certainly not the Communists from inside, and from outside not without a general conflict, in which case the general war emergency would offer remedies enough to combat such a danger without need of special legislation. Nationalists, on the other hand, able and resolved to carry out a *coup d'état* on their own account do not exist. On the assumption, therefore, that there are no deliberate anti-democrats in the government and parliamentary circles responsible for this initiative, the reference to a "gap" in our Basic Law which makes no provision for an emergency and the call to "close" it can only be explained as a piece of illusory juristic and political perfectionism. At the moment any pre-Fascist tendencies arose, however, it would assume direct and real importance. If the danger of Fascist infection existed and legislation for an emergency situation was available for use, safeguards for its employment could no doubt be quickly evaded.

As the *French danger* cannot unfortunately be dismissed, it is in the interests of our young democracy, therefore, that such legislation—which in any case is superfluous—should not even be contemplated.

Fortunately, *journalism* in the Federal Republic, in newspapers and periodicals, on the radio and television and also in the news agencies is extraordinarily sensitive to any attempt to create tools for dealing with emergency situations which might endanger basic rights, even under the pretext of protecting them. In the Federal Republic journalism does not need to squander its forces in fighting on several fronts against declared enemies of the constitution; it can therefore serve the development and consolidation of democracy through positive criticism in quite a different way than was formerly possible in Germany when strife was continually becoming more radical.

In this the journalists have allies, not the least of whom are the *trade unions*. Their demand for an increasing say in affairs springs from two causes : firstly, the consideration that experience has taught us that if we wish to preserve freedom we can no longer afford to leave decisions on day-to-day politics, either exclusively as hitherto or even mainly, to a minority privileged through power or possessions, and secondly, the will to control by economic and democratic means, if possible to abolish, but at least to form an effective counter-weight to those neo-feudal forces in our society which in certain circumstances might become a danger to political democracy.

Among the most important demands which should be repeatedly raised until they are realised belongs the requirement of our political representatives that they should adapt their own work in a continuous process, with many already overdue improvements, to the needs of a society which in the most decisive frontier area of the world systems must prove not merely by economic and technical achievements that the pluralism of forces produces more useful and more worthy results. Parliamentarians' own conceptions of these can sometimes be improved on—by reference to lessons applicable both to the present and the future which can be drawn from past experiences.